foreword

I have known about Jersey Pottery for almost as long as I can remember. Back when I was living in Jersey, the Pottery had a strong identity with the local community and everyone supported their ideals, and I know from my personal experiences that to this day, this is still the case.

My personal attachment to Jersey Pottery began in 1997 when my wife and I held our wedding reception there; we were the first people to have Jersey Pottery open on a Sunday! The food was spectacular, from the creamy Jersey butter to the locally-caught fish, and I remain a loyal customer to Jersey Pottery today.

Although I no longer live in Jersey, I still consider it my home and I am enthralled to see that the strong food culture remains. In recent years we've re-evaluated the importance of locally sourced, seasonal food and this is fundamental to Jersey's identity. It is involved in everything from the island's geography and history to its social culture. I can remember fishing for mackerel, having barbecues on the beach and my mum's great cooking; I think a passion for food is instilled in you from birth when you live in Jersey.

To me, Jersey symbolises food and good meals, and that's not because I'm a glutton! When I am lucky enough to return to the island, I socialise with friends and, of course, I visit Jersey Pottery – it has become a gastronomic experience for me: quality food, great wines and a great location.

Buying locally and supporting the local community is so important and I would encourage everyone to follow this formula. A celebration of local ingredients such as there is within this book is essential.

Enjoy!

Graeme Le Saux

ress

English Wat

'Rorippa nasturtium-aquaticum' Watercress is a member of the mustar

It has been used as a me

'Homarus Gammarus' Lobster is a crustacean of the primitive

'Cancer Pagurus' Brown

'Salmo Trutta' Sea trout are from the same species as

'Cheddar Cheeses' are traditionally made on farms in South West England, Cheddar is

Oyster Box Beach Bar & Restaurant

ST BRELADE'S BAY

Voted as one of the top beaches in Europe, the Oyster Box is located just three metres from the beachside and offers premium casual dining in a cosmopolitan environment that combines superb cuisine with slick and unpretentious service, delivered with the utmost professionalism. There is also a fantastic beach side terrace for alfresco dining.

Crab Shack

ST BRELADE'S BAY

One of the newest ventures for Jersey Pottery is the Crab Shack at St Brelade's Bay which adjoins the Oyster Box. Here we offer a more casual dining experience with Shackertisers to share, fish 'n' chips, delicious barbecue ribs and, of course, Jersey Chancre crab as well as an ice-cream parlour on the boardwalk catering for all generations. With a great selection of Jersey flavours, it provides a welcome treat in the summer sun.

Open seven days a week with a fully licensed bar, the Crab Shack in St Brelade also offers the biggest play area in the island, the beach!

Castle Green

Castle Green is a gastro pub which is situated opposite Gorey Castle with stunning views of Mont Orgueil castle as well as the Royal Bay of Grouville. The pub is operated by Jersey Pottery as a restaurant serving fantastically fresh and vibrant food in a relaxed but chic atmosphere.

La Mare Wine Estate

La Mare Wine Estate is a privately owned house and venue, which Jersey Pottery is proud to associate itself with as a partner venue. As the sole caterers for La Mare, Jersey Pottery operates the Vineyard Restaurant as well as functions in the Winery and marquees.

The Vineyard Restaurant seats 50 guests with a maximum of 60 for a party on large tables. The Winery can hold 150 guests with a dance floor and 180 without, the two areas combined can seat 220 guests. The lawn can accommodate parties of up to 350 in a marquee.

Jersey Pottery Cafés

ST HELIER

The superb quality of food and range of produce offered at the Pottery Cafés makes them the obvious venue for daytime coffee and pastries, or lunch on the go. Serving over 1000 people every day in St Helier alone, as with all of its offerings, Jersey Pottery knows the provenance of all the ingredients used and strives to offer such a comprehensive variety that no one can leave empty handed.

HANDMADE HOMEMADE
RECIPES FROM JERSEY

Jersey Pottery est.1946

publishers

First published in 2009 by
Network Publishing Limited
Network House
28 Ballmoor
Celtic Court
Buckingham
MK18 1RQ
www.networkpublishingltd.com
www.yeschefmagazine.com

ISBN   978-0-9562661-0-1
Printed in England

Publisher:
Peter Marshall

Photographer:
Myburgh du Plessis

Design Director:
Philip Donnelly

Managing Editor and Art Director:
Shirley Marshall

Editor:
Samantha Jones

Recipes:
Tony Dorris
Ebonny Hall
Neil Miller
Doris Stocker

contents

Features

12   From kiln to table

16   Island chef

44   Jersey oysters

76   Jersey royals

94   Bass

204   Cooking at source

208   Black butter

210   Eventful catering

Recipes

20   Soups

32   Sushi

40   Starters and light dishes

78   Salads

82   Fish and crustaceans main dishes

116   Barbecue principles and dishes

128   Poultry, game and meat main dishes

144   Pasta dishes

152   Cheese

156   Desserts

190   Bread masterclass

200   Stocks, sauces and dressings

203   Ingredients, measurements and timings

214   Index of recipes

from kiln to table

From humble beginnings as a small tourist attraction, today's thriving Jersey Pottery has become a diverse organisation offering award-winning ceramics, superb dining experiences and first-class outside catering

In 1954, Clive and Jesse Jones purchased Jersey Pottery and helped it to become a much-loved tourist attraction producing beautiful ceramics for all to enjoy. After numerous successful years, the way in which Jersey Pottery worked required some reconsideration, as Clive and Jesse's grandson Jonathan explains: "We used to be catering for mainly tourists in Jersey. It was a honeymoon island after the war and considered rather exotic. It would be teaming with British holidaymakers in the summer, as it was so close to England and they didn't need to worry about language or currency. When the 1990s hit with the wonders of low cost airline travel, things changed and people had the luxury of going further afield, so the number of tourists was much lower."

Jersey Pottery needed something to offer to the locals as well as the tourists, and this came in the form of a café. "Originally we were literally offering cups of tea and Kit-Kats," explains Robert, also a grandson of Clive and Jesse's, "But that soon gained momentum and contributed tremendously to the way our organisation is shaped today."

The success of Jersey Pottery is thanks to the dedication of three generations of the Jones family who have worked tirelessly to retain an ethos of service excellence coupled with outstanding quality. Today, brothers Jonathan, Robert and Matthew Jones steer the organisation's daily development, ensuring that this ethos is maintained and helping Jersey Pottery to remain a firm fixture in the local community. They certainly have a lot to manage, with restaurants, cafés, outside catering (which you can read more about on page 210) and party planning all coming under the Jersey Pottery umbrella, not forgetting the ceramics, where everything began.

...ng director of the ceramics side of the organisation,
... everything from individual ramekin, roasters, flan dishes,
...ters and much more. These beautiful creations
...s and restaurants from Texas to Dubai – in the world's
... – with high-end products filling the shelves of stores such as
...Mason.

...enware, bone china, porcelain and cook-proof stoneware, the
...d-painted, hand-glazed, hand-thrown or decorated with transfer
... going into the kilns. Each clay fires to a different temperature and time;
...s a 36 hour cycle which includes an initial firing at 900 degrees centigrade
... a second firing after glazing to between 1135 and 1240 degrees centigrade.
...y get decorated with transfer designs they are fired again at 800 degrees
...entigrade for another eight hours. After this process the transfers are dishwasher proof,
heatproof and food-safe, and the dishes ready for the table.

The ceramics are organised by range, from the Mediterranean collection with
its juicy red vine tomatoes and shining purple aubergines, to the intricately painted
Botanical collection with its delicate, colourful flowers. The ranges cater for every taste
and occasion, but it's the Fruits de Mer line, with its characteristic seafood designs that
has captured the imaginations of many a high profile chef. "Rick Stein from Padstow
and Michel Rostang from Paris use the Fruits de Mer collection in their restaurants,"
says Jonathan. "The Fruits de Mer range is inspired by the wealth of seafood produce
available in Jersey. It all started when one of our restaurants was open through the spring
and summer; hundreds of people would come out here and have prawns and lobster
salad. There was such a demand for shellfish products we set about designing a range
from Jersey Pottery, and Fruits de Mer ceramics evolved."

Of course, it's not just seafood that proves popular among the Pottery's culinary
clients, with Summer Lodge hotel in Dorset using the Game Bird range because of its
position in the countryside and reputation for pheasant, and Paxton and Whitfield utilising
the Cheese collection to complement their products, to name just a few.

You will see a number of the stunning designs available throughout this book and
Jonathan's tip for combining the ceramics with food presentation is that sometimes less
is more. "Some of the dishes have such strong designs that it's nice to arrange the food
around the design so that it shines through, or maybe the plate could be subtly put in the
background so the design complements the food. Michel Rostang, for instance, likes to
use Jersey Pottery tableware as presentation plates, replacing the dishes with white-ware
on serving the food."

What's more, Jersey Pottery does not stop at producing ceramics; on popular
demand, Jonathan has developed ranges of melamine coaster and tablemats, glass
clocks and an array of textiles, all to complement the existing ranges.

*For full details of the various ranges, including the option to buy online, visit
www.jerseypottery.com and click on ceramics.*

Royal Channel Island Yacht Club

island chef

Introducing Tony Dorris, the chef responsible for overseeing all of the dishes in this beautiful cookery book

When London-born Tony Dorris first started at catering college aged 16, it's doubtful that he would have imagined one day living in Jersey and heading up the food offering for Jersey Pottery. But this is his reality, and his role as executive head chef for Jersey Pottery involves him overseeing the food at six restaurants, three cafés, two function venues, one school canteen, a yacht club and an event catering business that often requires him to cook for up to 800 people.

When it comes to food, Tony has certainly earned his credentials, cooking under the Jersey Pottery banner for almost two decades, everywhere from La Mare Wine Estate to the beach – catering for locals, holiday-makers and royalty alike. So how did he get here? "After a short spate as a fishmonger when I left school I realised that I wanted to work more closely with food, so I enrolled in a catering course at my local college." he says.

"I really fell for food after about a year. I went for a placement at Inigo Jones in the west end of London and that's when my love of restaurant kitchens began." After this, Tony worked his way around four hotel restaurants, including the Intercontinental on Grosvenor Square and the Royal Garden in London. At 22, he came to Jersey for the first time as a sous chef, before heading back to London for one final stint as a sous chef at the Ritz, after that joining the Jersey Pottery Garden Restaurant at 24.

17

"WE'VE COLLATED EVERYTHING FROM OUR OYSTER RECIPES TO MODERN MOROCCAN SOUP RECIPES, BUT THE EMPHASIS HERE IS ON WHAT PEOPLE WANT – SO WE'VE INCLUDED OUR PLATEAU DE FRUITS DE MER, OUR TEMPURA KING PRAWNS WITH SPICE MIXES FOR THE TEMPURA, OUR SUSHI, MUSSELS COOKED IN LOCAL CIDER AND SAFFRON, TO NAME A FEW."

"I've been involved in the evolution of the business from one restaurant into coffee shops, bars and outside catering – and this book is a reflection of the food we serve in all these different parts of the business," he explains. "They're our favourite recipes that we've produced over the years – the ones that people like and have tended to stay on the menu. It's a chance for our patrons to reproduce the food at home – from the breakfast pancakes we serve in Spinnakers to our garlic mayonnaise, which everyone raves about. It's all in here."

Fifteen years with one company is loyal by any chef's standards, but as Tony explains – the challenges of his job ensure he's never short of variety or momentum. "We're very versatile in what we do. There's something different everyday – one minute I'm on the pass at the Oyster Box, the next I'm doing a function for 800 people up at Fort Regent and that way of working fits me like a glove. We work in a very happy way – we need the food to go out to the best of our ability and though it's hard when you're catering for 800 people, the variety keeps you fresh."

But Jersey's wealth of fresh ingredients and superior produce has also been a major factor in Tony's staying power. "The style of food here and the produce that's available is part of the reason I stayed on the island," he says. "The food we do is very simple – we work with the ingredient rather than making fancy patterns around plates. It's about giving people simple food with quality ingredients that match each other. I'd say we're quite classically motivated in the way we produce things, traditional dishes served in a contemporary style."

Indeed, no one could accuse this chef of being set in his ways. If there's one thing being in charge of all these different food outlets has taught Tony, it's the art of reinvention, as he's constantly developing the food he's engineering. He also points out the influence he takes from other continents, with an Asian influence underpinning many of his dishes – like the brill baked in banana leaf with chilli.

"We have an abundance of local chilli here which is really nice, sweet and medium hot. Though we try and use as much Jersey produce as possible, it's a small island, so you've got to utilise things and styles of cookery from around the world. We do that, but twist them to be our own, and listen to what the customers want. We try and refine every recipe we have and are constantly developing and finding a better way of doing it."

So what sort of dishes can we expect from the pages of this cookbook? The simple, flavoursome recipes that define the food style of the Pottery, with everything from canapés to Thai curries made with local ingredients. "The recipes are simple and easy to follow," he says. "We've collated everything from our oyster recipes to modern Moroccan soup recipes, but the emphasis here is on what people want – so we've included our plateau de fruits de mer, our tempura king prawns with spice mixes for the tempura, our sushi, mussels cooked in local cider and saffron, to name a few."

Having grown up in south London, Tony still finds himself surprised by the food culture of the island, which he likens to that of its closest neighbour, France. "It's a food haven. The locals are knowledgeable about food because they've all lived from the earth. My wife is from Jersey and she's always been involved in fresh food – the locals have grown it and it's much closer to the way of living in France – the markets are there, they make their own fresh bread in the morning – I didn't get that in London, but here it's the way they live."

Tony is something of a cookbook fanatic (he professes to owning at least 500), and as a chef who is as comfortable barbecuing on beaches as he is cooking for the Royal family, a natural skill with ingredients and an affinity with flavours characterises the recipes on the following pages. So whether you're just whipping up a quick dish of local scallops and crispy bacon for one, or catering for a friend's party, you'll find what you need here.

"We don't work in a stuffy environment – it's about kicking your shoes off and having something really tasty and simple. Relax and enjoy it – a lot of our food has been adapted to be able to serve two to 800 people, so you'll find you can cater for anything."

19

watercress soup with poached jersey royal bay oysters and fresh horseradish

Serves 4 healthy servings

Ingredients:

1	small onion (finely chopped)
120g	leek (sliced)
1	clove garlic (peeled and sliced)
250g	potatoes (peeled and chopped fairly small)
1ltr	chicken stock
2	bunches watercress (washed and big stalks removed)
1 tsp	fresh horseradish and a little more to grate on top
12	Jersey Royal Bay Oysters (shelled and half the juice retained)
2 tbsp	olive oil
½	bay leaf
25g	unsalted butter
salt and pepper	

Method:

1. In a thick bottomed saucepan add the olive oil then over a moderate heat stir fry the onions, leeks and garlic without too much colour for about 5 minutes. Season with salt and pepper and add the horseradish and the bay leaf.
2. Cook for a further minute then add the potatoes and chicken stock. Bring to the boil and simmer for about 20 minutes until the potatoes are cooked. Remove the bay leaf, add the watercress and butter and liquidise. Return to the heat, add the oysters and as much of the juice as required to give it a nice consistency and taste. Check the seasoning.
3. After about 90 seconds on the heat without boiling, the oysters should be just about cooked.
4. Divide between 4 bowls, trying to get 3 oysters in each bowl. Sprinkle with a few retained watercress leaves and the grated horseradish if desired.

Chef's tip:

This dish is delicious with or without the oysters and is also nice with scallops.

Suggested wine:

Any white! Try a Chenin Blanc.

Illustration using
Bespoke ceramics for Oyster Box Jersey

sweet potato, pumpkin and mascarpone soup
Serves 4 to 6

Ingredients:

200g	fresh orange pumpkin (peeled and sliced)
200g	sweet potato (peeled and sliced)
1	clove of garlic (peeled and chopped)
1	small onion (peeled and sliced)
1	stick celery (peeled and sliced)
1	medium carrot (peeled and sliced)
1	medium potato (peeled and sliced)
¼	small red chilli (chopped)
1 ltr	chicken stock (see page 202 for recipe, or use a stock cube)
1	small bunch of fresh thyme
25g	Jersey butter
50g	mascarpone cheese
200ml	Jersey milk
salt and pepper	

Method:

1. Gently heat a heavy based saucepan and add the butter. When melted add the onions, garlic, celery, carrot and chilli and stir fry without much colour for 2-3 minutes. Then add the pumpkin and sweet potatoes and continue to stir fry.
2. Add the potato and cook for a further minute or 2 before adding the chicken stock. Season with a little salt and pepper and add the thyme. Bring to the boil and then simmer for 10 minutes. Add the milk and continue to simmer for a further 15 minutes. Check all the vegetables are cooked.
3. Remove from the heat and liquidise the mixture.
4. Return to the saucepan, adjust the seasoning, and whisk in the mascarpone. Add a little water if required.

To serve:

Serve in a warm bowl. Garnish with a small spoon of mascarpone cheese and a few coriander leaves if desired.

Illustration using
Jersey Pottery Partiri and Helix range

jersey crab chowder

Serves 4 or 6 for lunch

Ingredients:

200g	diced onion
25g	plain white flour
100g	smoked streaky bacon rind removed and diced
1 tbsp	olive oil
300g	picked white crab meat
75g	brown crab meat (optional, gives a deeper flavour)
400ml	Jersey milk
800ml	chicken stock (hot, see page 202 for recipe)
400g	potatoes (peeled and diced in ¼ inches)
100ml	Jersey whipping cream
1	clove garlic (chopped)

salt and ground white pepper

Method:

1. Heat the oil in a heavy based saucepan. Add the bacon and fry over a moderate heat for 2-3 minutes without too much colour. Add onions and garlic; continue to gently cook, again without too much colour, for a further few minutes until it softens.
2. Stir in the flour and cook for 2-3 minutes, again without too much colour.
3. Slowly add the stock (kept hot so as you pour it into the pan it incorporates easier) then add the milk and potatoes.
4. Season lightly with the salt and ground white pepper. Cover with a lid and cook until the potatoes are just cooked.
5. Stir in the crab and the cream.

To serve:

Serve in warm bowls. You could garnish the dish with picked coriander and if you like some heat, use some chopped chilli. If you want a stronger flavour, use the brown meat from the head of the crab (called the boat).

Suggested drink:

Chilled draught Warsteiner lager or our Fish Hoek Sauvignon Blanc.

Illustration using
Jersey Pottery Cook and Serve Fruits de Mer range

mexican spiced tortilla soup with jersey crab and coriander

Serves 4 to 6

Ingredients:

1	red onion (peeled and chopped)
2	cloves of garlic
40ml	olive oil
600g	tomatoes, very ripe
½	long red chilli (chopped)
2	6 inch tortillas (cut into thin strips)
800ml	chicken stock (see page 202 for recipe)
1	avocado (diced)
100g	fresh picked crab
50ml	sour cream
1	lime
25ml	vegetable oil
20	chives (chopped)

a few coriander leaves
salt and pepper

Method:

1. In a heavy based saucepan add half of the olive oil and gently heat. Add the onions and garlic and cook for a few minutes without colour.
2. Cut the tomatoes in half and lay them on a baking tray, sprinkle with salt and pepper and brush with the remainder of the olive oil. Place under the grill or in a hot oven and cook for 4-5 minutes until just starting to colour. Add the tomatoes to the onions and garlic, add the chillies and chicken stock, bring to the boil and cook for 20-30 minutes.
3. Blend in a liquidiser and pass through a sieve. Season with salt and pepper. Set aside.
4. Mix the crab with the sour cream and chopped chives and set aside.
5. Mix the vegetable oil with the tortilla strips and lay on a baking tray in a preheated oven (200°C) for 5 minutes, until the tortillas start to crisp. Turn them over and return to the oven to crisp all over. Drain on a kitchen towel before serving.

To serve:

Distribute the hot soup between four bowls and add the diced avocado. Spoon the crab on top of the avocado, place tortillas on the crab and sprinkle with coriander. Serve with a wedge of lime.

Suggested drink:

We would suggest a 'very' chilled Corona with a wedge of lime which would slip down gloriously with this spicy soup. For once, no wine necessary!

Illustration using
Bespoke ceramics for Oyster Box Jersey

27

chunky chicken, vegetable, pine kernel and ricotta soup

Serves 6 to 8

Ingredients:

1	small chicken (1.2kg)
3 tbsp	olive oil
1	small onion (finely chopped)
1	stick celery (peeled and finely chopped)
1	clove garlic
75g	leeks (chopped)
75g	carrots (peeled and chopped)
75g	swede (peeled and chopped)
75g	butternut squash (peeled and chopped)
75g	Savoy cabbage (washed and chopped)
50	pine kernels
100g	ricotta cheese
1	small bunch fresh thyme
1 tsp	lemon juice
salt and pepper	

Method:

1. Place the whole chicken in a saucepan and cover with water. Add the fresh thyme, a good pinch of salt, a little pepper and any vegetable trimmings you have. Bring the chicken to the boil then simmer for about 50 minutes.
2. Pull the pan to the side and leave the chicken in the liquid for a further 30 minutes. Remove the chicken from the liquid and check that the chicken is cooked, then leave it to cool. Pass the liquid through a strainer.
3. In a heavy based saucepan, heat 2 of the tablespoons of olive oil to a moderate heat then add the onion, celery, leeks, and garlic. Cook for 5 minutes without much colour and then add the remaining vegetables.
4. At this stage add a little salt and pepper and continue to cook for a further 5 minutes. Add sufficient stock to cover the vegetables and simmer for 30 minutes or until the vegetables are cooked.
5. Cut all of the chicken off the bone and dice it a similar size to the vegetables. Add the chicken to the soup, adding a little more stock if required.
6. Place the pine kernels on a baking tray and sprinkle them with a little salt. Drizzle a little olive oil over them and place in a preheated oven (190°C) for 5 minutes until lightly browned. Take care not to over cook them as they burn very quickly. Add the roasted pine kernels to the soup, stir in the ricotta cheese and simmer for a further minute or so. You may want to retain half of the ricotta to spoon on the soup at the last minute.
7. Add the lemon juice, check the seasoning and serve.

Suggested wine:

This dish would really suit a light Pinot Grigio Rosato. We love the 'blush' style such as the Ponte Pietra from the Veneto.

harira – moroccan style lamb and vegetable soup

Serves 4 to 6

Harira is traditionally served during Ramadan in Morocco to break the fast as daylight disappears because it is a very heavy, robust meal which fills you up after fasting for so long. The Moroccans serve it with dates, grilled flat bread, and the classic Moroccan spice mix, Harissa. The recipe can also be made with a cheaper cut of beef, instead of lamb.

We serve it in our cafés as part of our chunky soup range.

Ingredients:

1	red onion (peeled and chopped)
2	sticks celery (peeled and chopped)
1	medium carrot (peeled and chopped)
250g	lamb (diced small and seasoned with salt and pepper)
1 tsp	ground turmeric
1 tsp	paprika
1 tsp	ground cumin
½ tsp	ground coriander
good	pinch of saffron
good	pinch of cinnamon
good	pinch of ground ginger
good	pinch of ground black pepper
250g	chopped tinned tomatoes
250g	tinned chick peas (rinsed and drained)
100g	puy lentils (soaked for a few minutes and drained)
1ltr	water (or chicken stock if you prefer)
50g	vermicelli noodles
30ml	olive oil
	juice of 1 lemon
	salt
	a pinch of cayenne pepper
	fresh coriander

Method:

1. In a heavy based saucepan heat the olive oil to a moderate heat then add the lamb and gently fry until it has a little colour.
2. Add the onion, celery and carrot and continue to cook for a minute or so.
3. Add the turmeric, paprika, cumin, cinnamon, cayenne pepper, ginger, ground coriander, black pepper and saffron and cook for a minute or two. Add the tinned tomatoes and the water and bring to the boil.
4. Simmer for 1 hour, until the lamb becomes tender, and add the lentils. Cook for a further 15 minutes then add the vermicelli noodles and the chick peas and cook for a further 5 minutes.
5. Season with salt and pepper and finish with lemon juice to taste. Sprinkle with freshly chopped coriander if desired.

Suggested drink:

This is a wonderful winter warmer lunch, we would enjoy this with cleansing Hildon water from the Hampshire hills, followed by a tasty coffee, served as you like it.

Illustration using
Jersey Pottery Partiri and Helix range

sushi

Translated, sushi means vinegared rice

basic sushi rice

Makes 6 thin rolls or 3 thick rolls

Ingredients:

230g	sushi rice (Japanese short grain rice)
325ml	water
2 tbsp	sugar
2 tbsp	rice vinegar
1 tsp	salt

1 small piece kombu (dried) seaweed (optional)

Method:

1. Wash the rice under running water for at least 10 minutes. Occasionally rub the rice in your hands. The rice should be washed until the water runs clear.
2. Drain the rice and place it in a heavy based, stainless steel saucepan. Add the water, and kombu if using, cover and bring to the boil.
3. Once boiling turn the heat down and simmer until the water has evaporated, which should take 6 to 7 minutes.
4. When the rice is cooked, remove it from the pan and evenly distribute it on a flat china plate or wooden tray. Cover with a cloth or cling film and allow to cool.
5. In a small saucepan put the sugar, salt and vinegar and dissolve over a low heat. Do not allow the mixture to boil. Once the sugar has dissolved, remove from the heat and allow the mixture to cool.
6. When the rice and sugar/vinegar mixture are both cool, mix the two together. Then the rice is ready to work with.

To serve:

Sushi should be served as quickly as possible once made and should be eaten at room temperature, although it will last a day in the fridge.

sushi rolls

Sushi rolls, sometimes known as California rolls, are a great and easy way to eat sushi. They are perfect for a lunch or a first course for a dinner party, even a canapé! We sell sushi in all our restaurants, cafés and outside catering.

All you need to make sushi rolls is:

A bamboo rolling mat

Nori seaweed sheets

Wasabi paste

Prepared sushi rice

Fillings of your choice

Vinegared water to dip your hands in

32

FILLINGS

japanese omelette

Ingredients:

1   free range egg
1   free range egg yolk
1 tsp   cornflour (mixed with
        a drop of water until
        liquid)
1   pinch salt
1 tsp   vegetable oil

Method:

1. Mix all the ingredients together, apart from the oil. Using a standard omelette pan or other non stick frying pan, heat to a moderate heat and brush with vegetable oil.
2. Roll the egg mixture around the pan and cook for 40 seconds on the first side.
3. Turn over and cook the second side for 10 seconds without much colour, similar to a normal pancake.

fish marinade

Ingredients:

75ml   thin soy sauce
75ml   rice vinegar
50g   sugar

Chef's tip:

This makes a very good combination filling for sushi if layered on the rice with salmon on the omelette then rolled up.

fish for sushi

For obvious reasons, when using fish for sushi it needs to be as fresh as possible. We are extremely concerned about the type and quality of our fish, how and where it was caught or in the case of salmon, farmed; salmon is the only fish which we use that is farmed.

When we prepare fish for sushi fillings we use tuna and salmon fillets, and prepare a teriyaki type marinade, marinating the fish for approximately 20 minutes before searing it in a hot frying pan. We flash fry the fish, cooling it as quickly as possible then slicing it to the thickness required to make the rolled sushi.

You can find the unusual Japanese ingredients in oriental shops or the oriental section of supermarkets.

We also use different combinations of fillings including:

crab meat
prawns
pickled vegetables
pickled ginger
chives
Japanese omelette
cucumber
smoked salmon
smoked trout
avocado
green beans
roast capsicum

For example:

*   Crab meat with chopped chives, prawns and pickled vegetables
*   Seared salmon with cucumber strips, pickled ginger wrapped in omelette rolls
*   Make thinner rolls with just one ingredient, such as seared tuna (serve seared tuna sliced thinly, like carpaccio)
*   Even a neutral mayonnaise brushed on salmon or avocado is a nice filling

We take a western approach when preparing sushi and don't serve the fish completely raw as they do in Japan. As with all our dishes, we listen to the customers and adapt our recipes to suit their needs.

TO SERVE THE SUSHI YOU WILL NEED:

wasabi

Wasabi is known as Japanese horseradish. It is very pungent and although we love it, some people find that it is just too hot. There are three ways to buy wasabi,

1. In its root form – which can be quite difficult to obtain outside Japan.
2. Ready mixed tubes of wasabi – very convenient, but once opened it can lose its kick.
3. Powdered wasabi – easy to keep in the cupboard and has a long shelf life, it also hold its flavour well (mix 1 tablespoon of wasabi powder to 1 tablespoon of water. Allow to sit for 5 minutes to develop its flavour).

We use both ready mixed tubes and powdered wasabi. We find the tubes are convenient for what we need and they suit the Western palette as they are not too fiery.

soy sauce

There are many different types of soy sauce on the market. We use a light soy sauce for the marinades and a dark Japanese style soy sauce for dipping. With some of our sushi platters we serve a pot of soy sauce with wasabi also inside the dish. Japanese style soy sauce is more fragrant.

pickled ginger

We use pickled ginger in some of our sushi rolls but it normally has its place as an accompaniment to sushi. It cleanses your palate between mouthfuls so you can taste the next flavour and is also very good for your immune system, and it aids digestion.

hand formed sushi – nigri

These are little balls of sushi moulded into an oval shape, usually around a piece of skinless raw fish. First make a few sushi balls, bite size, and then thinly slice pieces of fish at an angle. Brush a little wasabi on to the fish and mould it around the rice using your thumb and index finger.

making sushi rolls

Make a bowl of vinegared water (2 tbsp rice vinegar/250ml water) to keep your hands clean while making the rolls.

1. Place your rolling mat on a chopping board or flat surface. Lay a sheet of cling film on the sushi mat (this keeps it clean and when your sushi roll is done it's already in cling film).
2. Lay a sheet of nori (dried seaweed sheet) with the shiny side facing downwards.
3. Dip your hands into vinegared water; take the rice to almost cover the sheet of nori, leaving a little edge at the top and the bottom of the sheet.
4. Run a very thin line of wasabi along the centre of the roll.
5. Then arrange a filling on top of the wasabi. This could be a strip of salmon or tuna, or your favourite combination of fillings.
6. Lift the mat up and away from you, rolling round to make the two sides of the nori meet.
7. Roll the mat over to get a nice roll.
8. Use vinegared water to wet the knife between slicing the rolls.
9. Slice the rolls and arrange on a plate. Serve with wasabi, soy sauce and pickled ginger.

Chef's tip:
To make the thinner rolls simply cut the nori sheets in half down the centre and make the fillings smaller in size. It's nice to serve a combination of small and large sushi rolls and the small rolls make great canapés.

inside out rolls (ISO)

To make these rolls (often seen on sushi plates coated in tobiko – fish eggs – or toasted sesame seeds).
Simply take the rolled sushi to stage 3 above, and then flip them over placing the filling directly onto the nori sheet. Roll the sushi inside out. This will work especially well with the more moist fillings such as avocado mayonnaise or crab mixed with a little wasabi and ginger mayonnaise.

Method:
1. Mix the wasabi powder with equal amounts of water. Grate the ginger so there are approximately 2 teaspoons of juice (discard the pulp).
2. Mix the ginger juice, wasabi and mayonnaise together.

Chef's tip:
This works well with oily fish and will last approximately a week in the fridge.

ginger wasabi mayonnaise

This is a good sushi dip for the Western palate and is also great to help flavour fillings for the rolled sushi.

Ingredients:

4 tsp   wasabi powder
20g   fresh root ginger (peeled)
175g   good quality mayonnaise

Suggested wine:
Villa Maria or Cloudy Bay Sauvignon Blanc will suit this superbly. We're very lucky to have one of the largest Cloudy Bay Sauvignon Blanc allocations in the UK.

Season: Summer

masterclass: sushi

1. Rinse rice until water runs clear.

2. Bring to boil and simmer for 7 minutes to cook.

3. Lay cooked rice on a plate or tray and allow to cool.

4. Prepare filling for sushi rolls.

1

2

3

4

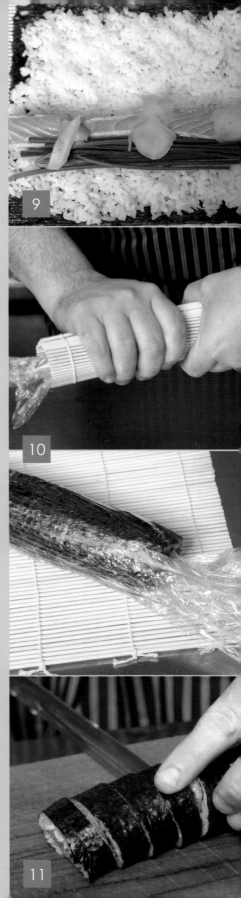

5. Lay nori sheet on bamboo rolling matt.

6. Spread out prepared sushi rice onto nori sheet.

7. Lay filling onto centre of the rice.

8. Build up extra fillings.

9. You are now ready to roll.

10. Use your rolling matt to create perfect cylinder.

11. Now it's ready to cut.

blinis

To be served as canapés

Makes approximately 24 small blinis

This is a lighter version of the classic buckwheat recipe. We still use the buckwheat flour variety in certain circumstances, as it does go well with caviar and is a good alternative for the Celiac diet. We regularly use blinis as a canapé usually piping a little cream cheese and chive mixture, then adding either smoked fish or caviar.

Ingredients:

175g	strong flour
1 tsp	sugar
1 tsp	salt
100g	unsalted butter (melted)
2	egg yolks
10g	yeast
210ml	warm milk
2	egg whites (whisked)

Method:

1. Mix the yeast with the flour, sugar and salt. Heat the butter until melted, pour onto the milk then mix with the dry mix and leave in a warm place for about ¾ hour until the mixture is bubbling and quite warm.
2. Fold in the egg whites and the blini mix is ready to cook.
3. To cook, heat a large non stick frying pan to a moderate heat and add a little vegetable oil. Then add a full dessert spoon of the blini mixture. Cook for 2 minutes on the first side and then turn them over and cook for 30 seconds on the other side.
4. Alternatively you can fill a medium size frying pan filled to about ½ inch, then once cooked it can be turned over and then cut with a cutter.

Suggested wine:

It's got to be champagne!

Season: Late Spring / Early Summer

jersey asparagus with poached quails' eggs and pecorino sabayon

Serves 4 as a starter or light lunch

Ingredients:

24	medium Jersey asparagus tips
4	egg yolks
100ml	Marsala
100ml	Jersey double cream
75g	grated Pecorino
12	quails' eggs
75ml	white wine
50ml	white wine vinegar
2	shallots
75g	Jersey unsalted butter
40ml	olive oil

juice of ½ a lemon
salt and freshly ground black pepper

Suggested wine:

It has to be Sancerre with this dish. Crisp, sharp citrus is all you need to complement the asparagus and the richness of the butter.

Method:

1. Bring a pan of well salted water to the boil (just enough to cover the asparagus).
2. Break the woody base of the asparagus away, this should just snap in your hands, then peel the asparagus from the bottom of the tip down if you desire.
3. Blanch the asparagus by dropping them into the water; this should take approximately 2 minutes. The asparagus will be barely cooked, and needs to be cooled down quickly, so plunge the spears into a bowl of cold water containing ice. When the asparagus is cold, drain and set to one side.

to make the sabayon:

1. Whisk the egg yolks, ½ teaspoon of freshly ground black pepper and Marsala together for 3 minutes or until it becomes frothy. Place the bowl over simmering water and continue whisking while the egg gently cooks and becomes thick, so you can almost draw a picture with the mixture using your whisk.
2. Place the bowl over ice and whisk until its cold. This will take 3-4 minutes.
3. Whisk the cream until it is just firm.
4. Carefully fold the cream into the sabayon as well as half the cheese, a pinch of salt and refrigerate until ready to serve.

to poach the quails' eggs:

1. Bring a saucepan half full of water to a gentle simmer, add a pinch of salt and 20ml of the vinegar. Crack the eggs into individual pots ready to poach.

to make the lemon shallot butter:

1. Melt a little of the butter in a saucepan, add the shallots and fry over a medium heat, without colour, for 2 minutes.
2. Raise the heat, add the white wine and remaining vinegar and reduce until the liquid is almost evaporated.
3. Reduce the heat and whisk the butter into the liquid creating a melted butter sauce. Finish with lemon juice, salt and pepper.
4. Set aside in a warm place.

to assemble the dish:

1. In a non stick frying pan, gently heat the olive oil. Add the asparagus, carefully laying it out over the pan, and season with salt and pepper. Heat the asparagus through gently without adding colour.
2. Returning to your pan of water, swirl the water with a slotted spoon to make the water move before you submerge your eggs. This will help them stay together. Drop the eggs into the water one by one, starting at one edge of the pan and working your way around the edge of the pan. The reason for this is so that when you return to the first egg it will be cooked.
3. The eggs will take approximately 2 minutes. When the eggs are cooked, lift them out and drain them on a cloth.
4. Put 6 spears of asparagus onto each plate, with 3 quails' eggs lying on top of them. Spoon a little lemon shallot butter over the quails' eggs and a large spoonful of sabayon over the asparagus. Sprinkle with the remaining cheese and cracked pepper.

jersey oysters

Gracing restaurant menus from Cancale to Dubai, Jersey oysters have never had a stronger reputation

The Noisette Oysters served up at Jersey Pottery's Oyster Box restaurant are supplied by Royal Bay Fisheries Ltd. A relatively small site, it's hard to believe that Royal Bay sorts through 25 million oysters a year, but then Jersey exports 750 tonnes of the molluscs annually – almost as much as the whole of the UK.

Alex Navarre, part owner, spent five years studying oysters and marine agriculture at university, he worked at Kermaree – one of the largest oyster distributors in France – before coming to Jersey. He believes his oysters are very good quality because the currents from the Gulf Stream bring in excellent food and nutrients, producing plump, fast growing oysters.

Noisette oysters are a slightly different thing to your average rock oyster. Smaller in size, these oysters are plucked from their sea-engulfed slumber at the young age of ten months, giving them a sweet, tangy flavour and a unique colour: perfect with a nice glass of white wine as an aperitif.

The seed oysters are brought in from France and planted in growing bags down on the seabed. From here it takes them around ten months to grow into Noisettes and 18 months to two years to full-sized oysters.

The original founder of Royal Bay Fisheries, Doug Le Masurier, was one of the first to start producing oysters commercially 20 years ago. "From a grower's point of view, oysters are easy to grow here," he says. "They grow fast because the number of oysters in this bay is quite small so the demand on the food content and water is low, and therefore the oysters are getting plenty of flow. There's a very big flow of current through

the bay here and big rise and fall of tides, which tends to give us a bit more time for working on the beach.

The oysters have a thick, heavy shell, and the meat content is high – the flavour is great. Each oyster's flavour is different because it'll take the flavour from the water it's in. In a similar way, Navarre explains that the oysters contain a molecule that changes colour according to its environment – thus taking on the colour of the rocks that surround them.

For the final, crucial stage of the production process, the oysters are moved to a cleansing and holding area where they are left to rid them of any sediment and conditioned to stay shut. When they come out of the growing area, they've been in water for five to six weeks and are open because they have been feeding continuously. In the holding area they are in water for six hours and out for six hours, which teaches them to stay shut, keeping them moist inside and giving them a shelf-life of eight days

When you see the oyster beds stretching out for miles, like train tracks leading into the sea, it's easy to see why Jersey is such a hub for oyster production. But this is by no means intensive farming, as the beds are generously spaced out metres from each other and it's precisely this spacious approach that makes them a superior product. "We could triple what we've got but haven't done that and that's why we get good, fast growth and good oysters," explains Navarre.

45

royal bay oysters kenney-herbert

Serves 4 as a starter

This oyster dish was named after a regular Jersey Pottery customer and friend, Mike Kenney-Herbert, an Australian sheep farmer turned financier and foodie. This recipe is the classic 'Oysters Kilpatrick' found on many Australian menus, which we have adapted slightly.

Ingredients:

24	No2 Royal Bay oysters (opened, tops removed and oyster separated from the base of the shell)
200g	bacon lardons or pancetta (lightly pre-cooked in a frying pan)
2	lemons
6 tbsp	tomato sauce (see 'Basic tomato sauce' recipe below. Tomato Ketchup can be used instead, but it can be a little sweet)
6 tbsp	Worcester sauce
150g	Gruyere cheese (grated)
coarse salt	

Method:

1. Set the oysters on bed of coarse salt on a tray (or on small tin foil rings on a tray).
2. Sprinkle the bacon over the oysters.
3. Blend the Worcester sauce and the tomato sauce together and top each of the oysters with a small amount of the combined sauce.
4. Sprinkle each oyster with Gruyere cheese and pop under a hot grill for 3-4 minutes or bake in a pre-heated oven at 210°C for 4-5 minutes.
5. Sprinkle coarse salt on 4 plates and place the oysters on the salt for stability when serving.
6. The oysters need to be eaten straight from the grill, piping hot.
7. Serve with lemon wedges and the rest of the sauce.

basic tomato sauce

Ingredients:

300g	ripe tomatoes, quartered
30g	tomato puree
1	small red onion (diced)
1	sprig of thyme
1	bay leaf
1	clove of garlic (roughly diced)
75ml	dry white wine
1 tbsp	olive oil
salt and pepper	

Method:

1. Heat the olive oil in a saucepan; add the onions, garlic and herbs then the tomato puree. Cook for a minute or so then add the white wine.
2. Reduce until the liquid has evaporated then add the tomatoes. Season with salt and pepper.
3. Cook for 25-30 minutes on a low heat. Remove the herbs, liquidise and pass through a sieve before serving.

Suggested drink:

Dry Reisling from the Great Southern region of Southern Australia, or Guiness.

Illustration using
Jersey Pottery Partiri and Helix range

47

grilled oysters with chorizo butter

Serves 4

Ingredients:

24	oysters (opened)
75g	soft Jersey unsalted butter
75g	cooking chorizo (chopped to ¼ inch diameters)
1	small bunch flat parsley (roughly chopped)
2	garlic cloves (finely chopped)

pinch of curry powder
grated zest of half a lemon
salt and pepper

Method:

1. Place the parsley, butter, garlic and a pinch of curry powder in a food processor and pulse until the parsley is completely ground down.
2. Season with a little salt and pepper and the lemon zest. Beat in the chorizo.
3. Set in the fridge in either a terrine mould or in a plastic container until firm.
4. Dice the butter into small pieces ready for the oysters.
5. Place the oysters on a bed of coarse salt and add a small piece of the chorizo butter on top of each oyster. Place them under a hot grill for 2-3 minutes or until the oysters start to become firm. Make sure the oysters are fully cooked as warm raw oysters do not taste great!

Chef's tip:

This recipe can be adapted for barbecue cookery. Simply follow each step until you place the butter on the oysters and then place them onto a barbecue bar (of a well burnt barbecue). They will take approximately the same amount of time, 3 minutes, cooking them from underneath.

Suggested wine:

Chardonnay, Russian River Ranches, Sonoma Cutrer.

oysters with sweet vinegar, cucumber and chilli

Ingredients:

24	Royal Bay Oysters
6 tbsp	rice vinegar (white wine vinegar could be used as a substitute)
2 tbsp	caster sugar
1 tbsp	lemon juice
2 tbsp	diced cucumber
1 tsp	chopped green chilli
2 tbsp	shredded coriander
2	shallots (finely chopped)
1 tsp	salt

Method:

1. Place the vinegar, sugar and salt in a saucepan and dissolve over a moderate heat.
2. Allow the mixture to cool and mix in the other ingredients.
3. Open the oysters and set them on a tray of crushed ice.

To serve:

Serve with a pot of the vinegar, cucumber and chilli or spoon the vinegar into each oyster.

Suggested drink:

A Loire white such as Muscadet De Sevre et Main Sur Lie.

Royal Bay Noisettes of Jersey

These are premium miniature oysters that are best served as an aperitif with a glass of champagne. The light, delicate flavour makes them a favourite with even those who professed not to like oysters. Grown in Jersey by the Royal Bay Fisheries Ltd.

51

mussels with local cider, saffron and jersey cream

Serves 4 as a starter

Ingredients:

1kg	mussels
3	shallots (finely chopped)
1	clove of garlic (finely chopped)
20	threads saffron
50ml	white wine
75ml	Jersey cider from La Mare Wine Estate
75ml	Jersey whipping cream
1 tbsp	Ricard
1 tbsp	chopped parsley
1 tbsp	olive oil
salt and pepper	

Method:

1. Prepare the mussels by pulling the beard away, ensuring that the mussels are firmly closed. Discard any broken mussels and scrape away any barnacles.
2. Rinse the mussels under cold flowing water for a few minutes, drain in a colander and the mussels are now ready to cook.
3. Heat a heavy based saucepan to a moderate to hot heat. Add the olive oil, the shallots and garlic. Stir for a few seconds then add the mussels and the saffron.
4. Stir the mussels, add the white wine and the cider and place a lid on the pan. Turn the heat to full and cook for approximately three minutes, shaking the pan regularly.
5. When all the mussels are open, remove from the heat and add the cream, Ricard, parsley and season with salt and pepper.

To serve:

Serve with Jersey cabbage loaf or crusty French bread.

Suggested drink:

La Mare Pompette Jersey cider,
Loire white or any Sauvignon Blanc.

Season: Best Spring / Summer

praires farcies
small clams stuffed with parsley and garlic breadcrumbs

This is a most delicious light lunch, early supper or a great first course.

We are spoilt in Jersey with shellfish and when these clams come onto the fish market they don't stay on the counter for very long!

Praires are also known as 'Warty Venus' clams, but for obvious reasons we use the French name! Jersey fishermen will also refer to them as ridge clams. They are found in large quantities around the Jersey coast, especially the east and south coasts.

The French would serve these raw as part of a Plateau Fruits de Mer, but we tend to cook them. They have a wonderful delicate flavour.

Ingredients:

1kg	praires
80g	shallots (chopped)
3	cloves of garlic (crushed)
100ml	dry white wine
120g	white breadcrumbs
4 tbsp	flat parsley (chopped)
100g	soft unsalted butter
2 tbsp	olive oil
salt and pepper	

This also works well with cockles and amandes (dog cockles), all available from around Jersey's coast.

Method:

1. First plunge the praires into a bowl of cold water and soak for 10 minutes, repeat this process at least 2 more times and then drain the praires in a colander for 5 minutes.

2. To open the praires, hold a cloth in your hand and place the praire with the rounded edge upright. Slide a small knife inside and twist it, opening the praire, but trying not to cut into it, brush off any shell or sand and lay the half shell with the praire inside onto a baking tray and set aside.

3. In a saucepan heat the olive oil over a moderate heat, add the shallots and fry for a minute or 2 without much colour. Add the garlic and the white wine. Reduce until almost evaporated, then whisk in the butter, remove from the heat, add ¾ of the breadcrumbs and parsley and season with the salt and pepper.

4. Spoon a little of the mixture into each of the praires, sprinkle the remainder of the breadcrumbs on the praires and place in a preheated oven (210°C) for 5 minutes. The breadcrumbs should start to brown and the butter should start to bubble. The praires should be just cooked but still succulent.

Chef's tip:

To make the white breadcrumbs, just take white bread, even if it is starting to stale, cut the crusts off and place them into a food processor. Blend for 20 seconds until it becomes a coarse crumb.

Suggested wine:

Sauvignon Blanc or Rosé in the summer.

jersey spider crab cakes with 'shack attack' sauce

Serves 4

Chancre crab (brown crab) meat can also be used in this recipe, but where possible and when in season we like to use spider crab as it has a sweeter flavour.

Ingredients:

300g	spider crab meat
150g	pureed potatoes, or crushed, cooked Jersey Royals
5g	coriander and parsley (chopped)
250g	flour
1 tsp	Dijon mustard
2	eggs
150g	dry breadcrumbs (see chef's tip, page 54), mixed with 2 tbsp of chopped mixed herbs (we use parsley, tarragon and chervil)

Juice of ½ lemon
100ml Jersey milk
2 spring onions
1 tbsp olive oil
salt and pepper

'shack attack' sauce
From the Crab Shack,
St Brelade's Bay

Ingredients:

200ml	water
4 tbsp	sugar
4 tbsp	rice vinegar
4 tbsp	tinned tomato
1 tbsp	red chilli (chopped)
1 tsp	salt
½ tsp	ground white pepper

Method:

1. Mix the crab meat and potatoes with lemon juice, olive oil, spring onions, 2 egg yolks and Dijon mustard. Divide the mixture into 12 small flat cakes using floured hands. If the mixture is a little soft, leave in the refrigerator for 20 minutes.
2. Dip the cakes in egg whites and a little milk and then in herb breadcrumbs.
3. Heat some vegetable oil in a frying pan and place cakes in for about 4-5 minutes, turning constantly.
4. Drain on kitchen paper and serve with a salad garnish and 'Shack Attack' sauce.

Method:

1. Place all the ingredients into a saucepan and bring to the boil. Reduce by half.
2. Blend for about 5 seconds and add more chilli if you like it hot.

Suggested wine:

You have to go against the grain and choose a Chenin Blanc!

57

pottery prawns

Serves 4 as a snack or first course

Ingredients:

450g	peeled raw prawns (approx 16 prawns)
100-150g	dried breadcrumbs
2 bsp	salt
50g	desiccated coconut
2 tbsp	finely chopped fresh flat leaf parsley
2 tbsp	chopped fresh coriander
1 tbsp	finely chopped chervil
2	free range eggs (beaten)
600ml	ground nut or vegetable oil (for deep frying)

plain flour for dusting

'shack attack' sauce
From the Crab Shack,
St Brelade's Bay

150ml	water
4 tbsp	sugar
4 tbsp	rice vinegar
4 tbsp	tomato puree
1 tbsp	red chilli (chopped)
1 tsp	salt
¼ tsp	ground white pepper

Method for the prawns:

1. Wash the prawns in salted water and drain on a paper towel.
2. Whilst the prawns are drying, mix the breadcrumbs with the chopped herbs and desiccated coconut.
3. Next flour the prawns and shake off any excess, then dip in the beaten egg and then into the breadcrumb mixture. The prawns are now ready to either deep-fry or bake.
4. Serve with wedges of lime and the dipping sauce.

Method for the sauce:

1. Put all the ingredients into a saucepan and bring to the boil. Reduce by half.
2. Blend for about 5 seconds and add more chilli if you like it hot.

Suggested wine:

Through our suppliers we have sourced a wonderful Sauvignon Blancs from South Africa which we believe complements the style of the Oyster Box. We have sourced two ranges, Fish Hoek for Oyster Box and Franshhoek for Crab Shack. We firmly believe that the quality of our house wines reflect the quality of the restaurants. Either of these Sauvignon Blancs would complement this crispy prawn dish. Alternatively, a very cold lager would be perfect.

Illustration using
Jersey Pottery Partiri and Helix range

asian fish cakes with mango and chilli salsa

Serves 12 as a starter or 24 as canapés

for fish cakes

Ingredients

3	medium red chillis (diced)
1	shallot (finely chopped)
2	garlic cloves (peeled and chopped)
¼	bunch of coriander (chopped)
1 tbsp	galangal (alternatively, ginger)
3	kaffir lime leaves (finely chopped)
400g	minced fish (king prawns, and white fish, and even a little salmon would be a good mix, mince the fish for only a few seconds in a blender)
1 tbsp	fish sauce
60g	green beans (sliced very thinly)
1	lime (juice and zest)

Method:

1. Pound the chillis, shallot, garlic, coriander, galangal, lime leaves and salt with a pestle and mortar to form into a paste.
2. Place the minced fish into a mixing bowl and add the paste, green beans, fish sauce and zest of lime. Mix together.
3. Make the fish cake mix into balls. Allow to rest in the refrigerator for about 15 minutes then flatten them into little cakes with the palm of your hand. Allow to set in the refrigerator for about 1 hour.
4. To cook the cakes, heat a non stick frying pan to a moderate heat and add a little vegetable oil. Place the fish cakes in the pan and fry for about 2 minutes on the first side and then turn them over and cook for a further 1 minute on the other side. Drain them on a kitchen towel.

for the mango and chilli salsa:

Ingredients

1	mango
½	red chilli
1	shallot
1 tbsp	rice vinegar
1 tbsp	sugar
3 tbsp	water
1 tbsp	chopped coriander

Method:

1. Peel the mango and dice into small pieces. Place any trimmings or off cuts in a saucepan with the vinegar, sugar and water and bring to the boil. Simmer for a few minutes, liquidise and allow to cool.
2. Mix with the shallots, chillis, chopped coriander and diced mango.

Chef's tip:

This recipe will make a generous amount of mango salsa that will keep in the fridge for up to a week.

for the dipping sauce:

Ingredients

175ml	rice wine vinegar
2 tbsp	sugar
¼	cucumber (peeled and diced)
1	small carrot (peeled and diced)
3	shallots (diced)
1	red chilli (finely diced)

Method:

1. Place the vinegar and sugar in a saucepan and bring to the boil.
2. Allow to simmer for 1 minute.
3. Remove from the heat; allow to cool slightly before adding all the remaining ingredients. Serve cold.

Suggested wine:
Gewurtzraminer from Hugel would be good.

To serve:

Place a spoon or two of the mango and chilli salsa on four plates and place the fish cakes on top. Spoon the dipping sauce around the plate or serve in a pot on the side. Serve with a few coriander leaves and lime wedges if desired.

lightly cured salmon and avocado tians with fresh tomato and basil dressing

Serves 4

Ingredients:

350g   salmon fillet (skinned)
100g   smoked salmon
1   clove garlic (finely chopped)
3   shallots (finely chopped)
1½ tbsp   lemon juice
½ tsp   salt
12 turns black pepper mill
2   small avocados
½   lemon (to serve, optional)
pinch cayenne pepper
few drops of Worcester sauce
mixed salad leaves to garnish

for the dressing

Ingredients:

3 tbsp   extra virgin olive oil
1 tbsp   lemon juice
2   tomatoes (skinned and finely chopped)
½ tsp   coarse sea salt
8   leaves basil (coarsely chopped)
black pepper

Method:

1. Thinly slice the salmon fillet and smoked salmon and place them in a bowl with the garlic, shallots, 1 tablespoon of lemon juice, salt, black pepper, cayenne pepper and Worcester sauce. Mix together well.
2. Halve the avocados and remove the stones and peel. Cut each half into thin slices, then mix in the remaining lemon juice and a pinch of salt.
3. Place a 3 ½ inch poaching ring or plain pastry cutter in the centre of each of four large plates.
4. Divide half of the salmon mixture between the rings and lightly level the top without pressing the mixture down.
5. Cover each with avocado slices and the remaining salmon mixture and carefully remove the rings.
6. Lightly stir the dressing ingredients together in a bowl.

To serve:

Arrange four small piles of salad around each tian, spoon pools of dressing between the leaves and serve with half a grilled lemon if desired.

Suggested wine:

Fish Hoek Sauvignon Blanc, our house wine!

1. Ingredients for samosa filling.

2. Fry the filling.

masterclass: samosas

3. The cooked filling.

4. Cut the spring roll pastry to the appropriate size.

5. Brush the pastry with a little water or beaten egg.

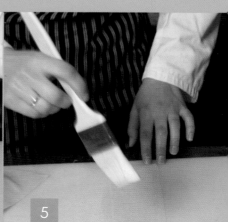

6. Fork the filling onto the pastry square.
7. Fold the pastry into triangles, ensuring you seal in the mix by leaving no gaps.
8. Repeat process.
9. Fry at 175°C for 3 minutes in total.
10. Serve on a platter with a pot of mint yoghurt dip.

indian style samosas with a mint yoghurt dip

Makes 20 samosas, canapé size

Ingredients:

200g	diced lamb (neck fillet with most of the fat removed, diced fairly small)
30g	diced onion
1 tsp	coriander seeds (roasted and coarsely crushed)
1 tsp	cumin seeds (roasted and coarsely crushed)
1 tbsp	medium curry powder
½ tsp	grated ginger
40g	diced butternut squash
1	clove garlic (crushed)
1 tbsp	diced mango
1 tsp	red chilli
1 tsp	salt
1 tbsp	corn oil
3 tbsp	tinned tomato
250ml	chicken stock (see page 202 for recipe)

zest of ½ lemon

3 tbsp	chopped coriander
1	packet of spring roll paste (available in Asian shops and some supermarkets)

good pinch of pepper

Method:

1. Heat the oil in a heavy based pan. Season the lamb with the salt and pepper and add to the pan. Fry until lamb is browned (about 3 minutes).
2. Add the onions and cook for a further 2 minutes then add the crushed coriander seeds, crushed cumin seeds, curry powder, chilli, garlic and ginger and cook for one more minute.
3. Add the tomatoes and chicken stock. Bring to the boil and simmer for about 30 minutes until most of the liquid has evaporated. Stir in the butternut squash and add 100ml of water. Cook for a further 10-15 minutes until the butternut squash and lamb are tender.
4. Add the lemon zest, chopped coriander and diced mango. Season with salt and pepper. Allow to cool, ready to roll into samosas.

mint yoghurt dip

Ingredients:

150ml	natural yoghurt
3 tbsp	chopped mint
1 tbsp	lemon
½ tsp	mint sauce

Method:

Mix all the ingredients together to make the dip.

Suggested drink:

Tiger Beer or Cobra.

grilled jersey spring vegetables with coriander pistou and yoghurt dressing

Serves 4 as a starter

Ingredients:

2	aubergines (each sliced into 6 or 8 and brushed with olive oil)
2	red peppers
4	courgette flowers (cut in half)
2	plum tomatoes (cut in half), or vine cherry tomatoes
1	red onion (cut into wedges)
1 tbsp	balsamic vinegar
1 tsp	sugar
coarse salt	

Method:

1. Cut the peppers in half and brush them with olive oil. Season with salt and pepper and place on a baking tray. Place in a preheated oven (200°C) for 10 minutes or so, until they have slightly blackened.
2. Remove them from the oven and cover them with cling film for 5 minutes enabling, you to remove the skin from the pepper easily.
3. Peel the peppers and cut them into strips.
4. Lay the red onions on a tray, sprinkle with sugar and balsamic vinegar and cook at 200°C for 15 minutes in a preheated oven.
5. Heat a griddle pan. Season the aubergine with salt and pepper and place in a grill pan. Griddle for 3 minutes each side over a moderate heat.
6. Remove and mix with the peppers.
7. Grill the tomatoes and courgette flowers, brushing with oil and seasoning with salt and pepper as you go.

yoghurt dressing

Ingredients:

150ml	natural yoghurt
2 tbsp	milk
50ml	olive oil (plus some for brushing)
zest and juice of 1 lemon	
salt and pepper	
1 tbsp	chopped parsley
2	cloves garlic

Method:

1. Brush the garlic with olive oil and roast with the skins on for 15 minutes at 180°C, then peel and crush.
2. Blend all the ingredients together, leaving the olive oil out.
3. Whisk in the olive oil at the end and check the seasoning.

coriander pistou

Ingredients:

100ml	olive oil
50g	coriander and basil (mixed)
20g	parmesan
salt and pepper	

Method:

1. Blend all the ingredients together in a food processor.

To serve:

Spread the yoghurt dressing on a plate. Mix the warm vegetables with Pistou and spread over the yoghurt dressing.

Suggested wine:

Pinot Grigio Sante Pietre or Gavi di Gavi.

Illustration using
Jersey Pottery Partiri and Helix range

69

braised chicory with garlic and parsley crust

This recipe is great served as a side dish or a starter, and is a great accompaniment to chicken and hearty fish dishes.

Ingredients:

4	heads chicory (Belgium endive)
1	bay Leaf
100ml	white wine
400ml	chicken or vegetable stock
½ tsp	orange zest
1 tbsp	orange juice
1 tbsp	olive oil
90g	white breadcrumbs (see chef's tip, page 54)
70g	grated parmesan
1 tbsp	chopped parsley
60g	unsalted butter (softened)
4	cloves garlic (chopped)
4 tbsp	stock from endive
2 tbsp	flat parsley (chopped)

salt and pepper

Suggested wine:

Chardonnay Ardéche, Louis Latour.

Method:

1. Cut the chicory in half. Brush a roasting tray with one tablespoon of the olive oil and place the chicory flat side down on the roasting tray, place over a moderate heat. Start to fry the chicory without too much colour then add the white wine and allow it to evaporate.
2. Add the chicken stock, the juice and zest of the orange and the bay leaf. Season with salt and pepper, cover with baking parchment and tin foil, then place in a preheated oven at 160°C for 50 minutes until the endive is soft but still has a bite to it.
3. Remove from the stock and retain some of the stock for the next stage.
4. Mix together the butter, garlic, stock from endive and parsley.
5. Brush 1 tablespoon of olive oil on a baking tray or frying pan and lay the chicory flat side down. Season with salt and pepper then spoon the butter mixture over the chicory.
6. Mix together the breadcrumbs, parmesan and parsley. Sprinkle this mixture over the butter mixture then place this into a preheated oven at 190°C for 25 minutes until the breadcrumbs are golden.

goats' cheese, red onion and tomato tart

These make a perfect light starter, or you can prepare them slightly smaller for canapés.

red onion compote

Ingredients:

200g	red onions (sliced)
75ml	red wine
50ml	red wine vinegar
150ml	water
pinch of salt	
2 tbsp	sugar

Method:

1. Place all the ingredients into a saucepan, bring to the boil and allow to simmer for 30 minutes or so on a low heat, stirring regularly, until all the liquid has evaporated and the mixture has softened and caramelised slightly.

tart

Ingredients:

120g	goats' cheese (St Maure is perfect for this recipe)
1	free range egg (beaten with a little milk)
1 tsp	thyme leaves
square of ready rolled puff pastry (16x16cm)	

Method:

1. Cut the puff pastry into 4. Brush with the egg wash and bake in a pre-heated oven at 190°C for 8-10 minutes. Remove from the oven, make a hole in the centre of each puff pastry, spoon the tomato sauce (see recipe below) in the centre of the puff pastry and place the onion compote on top. Slice the goats' cheese on top of that, sprinkle with a few thyme leaves and bake in the oven for 10 minutes at 190°C.
2. Dress with a little olive oil.

basic tomato sauce

Ingredients:

300g	ripe vine tomatoes, quartered
30g	tomato puree
1	small red onion (diced)
1	sprig of thyme
1	bay leaf
1	clove of garlic (roughly diced)
75ml	dry white wine
1 tbsp	olive oil
salt and pepper	

Method:

1. Heat the olive oil in a saucepan; add the onions, garlic and herbs then the tomato puree. Cook for a minute or so then add the white wine.
2. Reduce until the liquid has evaporated then add the tomatoes. Season with salt and pepper.
3. Cook for 25-30 minutes on a low heat. Remove the herbs, liquidise and pass through a sieve before serving.

Chef's tip:

These can be made a few hours before you need them and just re-heated in the oven at the last minute. They are nice as a first course or cut into smaller pieces as a canapé. For a starter you could spoon some rocket dressing around them and serve with a small amount of salad.

Suggested wine:

Pinot Noir, try putting it in the fridge for a couple of hours before drinking for the summer months.

scotch quails' eggs with curry mayonnaise

Serves 4 as a lunch, also good for canapés

Ingredients:

350g	pork sausage meat
1½ tbsp	chopped sage
1	small onion (finely chopped)
1	clove garlic (finely chopped)
100g	plain flour
2	eggs (beaten with 50ml milk)
100g	panko or white breadcrumbs (see chef's tip, page 54)
12	quail eggs
1 tbsp	olive oil
2 tbsp	white wine vinegar
salt and pepper	

Method:

1. In a saucepan heat the olive oil over a moderate heat, add the chopped onions and garlic and cook for 4-5 minutes without much colour. Remove from the heat and lay flat on a tray allowing to cool.
2. Mix the onion mixture with the sausage meat and sage then season with salt and pepper.
3. Place the quails' eggs in warm water for 20 seconds, this gets them used to a higher temperature and should prevent them from cracking, then plunge them into boiling water for 2 minutes and 20 seconds. Add the vinegar to a bowl of iced water and plunge the eggs into the water after cooking. When the eggs have chilled in the ice peel them carefully, taking care not to break the them. Dry them on a kitchen towel.
4. Taking the sausage meat, divide it into 12 pieces and roll it into balls. Flatten each ball with the palm of your hand and place a quail's egg in the middle of each piece of sausage meat. Wrap the sausage meat around the egg then roll the balls through the flour. Dust off all the excess flour before rolling the ball through the egg mixture. Then roll the sausage meat through the breadcrumbs brushing off all the excess.
5. Preheat the deep fat fryer, containing vegetable oil, to 165°C and cook the eggs for approximately 5 minutes. If using a kitchen probe, it should read about 68°C in the centre.
6. Drain on a kitchen towel.

curry mayonnaise

Ingredients:

250ml	good quality mayonnaise
1½ tbsp	curry paste (we use Sharwoods)
1/3 tsp	chilli powder
½	small red onion (chopped)
1	clove of garlic (chopped)
1 tbsp	vegetable oil
2 tbsp	mango chutney
salt and pepper	

Method:

1. In a frying pan gently fry the onions and garlic without too much colour for 3 minutes. Add the curry paste and chilli powder and season lightly with salt and pepper. Cook for 3-4 minutes.
2. Allow to cool then blend the spice mix with mayonnaise and mango chutney in a food processor.
3. Keep refrigerated for up to 2 weeks.

To serve:

Cut the scotch eggs in half and serve with a pot of the curry mayonnaise on the side.

Illustration using
Jersey Pottery Mediterranean range

jersey royals

The remarkable taste of Jersey Royals is recognised the world over. The distinctive, exceptional taste comes from the climate, the rich earth used for the crops and the growing expertise learned over generations of growing.

Jersey Royals have been grown on the island for over 100 years and there are at least 50 farmers who still solely produce the crop. Approximately six and a half thousand acres of the island's landscape is dedicated to the crop.

The main outdoor crop is planted from December/January with harvesting commencing in April and lasting until June. The activity peaks in May, when approximately one and a half tonnes of Jersey Royals are exported daily. The total annual yield ranges from 30 to 40 tonnes per year.

All the work to harvest the potatoes on the 'cotils', the steep sloping fields near the coast, is still carried out by hand. In keeping with this traditional practice, the 12th century custom of placing 'vraic' (seaweed) on the fields as a natural fertilizer is still performed today by some farmers.

Mainland Britain is where 99% of Jersey Royals are sold outside the island. They are subject to a stringent checking and quality control process, ensuring that they reach the supermarket shelves in the freshest conditions.

We use Jersey Royals because they are just the best tasting potato in the world, with the added benefit that they come from our beautiful island home.

greek style caesar salad

Ingredients:

6	quails' eggs (optional, cooking method on page 74, point 3)
1	pita bread cut into strips
3	little gem lettuce (heads, cut into quarters and core removed)
3	plum tomatoes (cut into quarters)
120g	feta cheese
1 tbsp	olive oil
coarse salt	

dressing

Ingredients:

20ml	tahini
100ml	yoghurt/fromage frais
½ tsp	Dijon mustard
50ml	olive oil
50ml	mayonnaise
handful of pitted green olives	
juice of ½ lemon	
pinch sugar	
salt and pepper	

Method:

1. Lay the tomatoes on a baking tray sprinkled with the coarse salt, skin side down. Place in a preheated oven at 100°C for about 1 hour. Slow baking the tomatoes will intensify the flavour.
2. Wash the salad and drain on a kitchen towel.
3. Mix the dressing with the salad and divide between 4 bowls.
4. Place the tomatoes on the salad, then sprinkle with crumbled feta. Place a few crispy pita pieces over the salad and add the quails' eggs, cut in half.
5. To make the pita bread pieces, brush the pita strips with olive oil and lay on a baking tray. Bake for 4-5 minutes at 200°C until crispy.

Method:

1. Mix all the ingredients together, leaving out the olive oil and the olives.
2. When ready to dress the salad, whisk in the olive oil.
3. Drizzle the dressing over the salad and top with the olives.

Suggested wine:

Chardonnay Ardéche, Louis Latour.

cobb salad

This is a typical salad that we serve in our cafés

Ingredients:

1	breast of roast chicken
2	slices crispy bacon (streaky is best)
¼	avocados
25g	crumbled blue cheese (stilton or blacksticks)
1	free range boiled egg (4 minute boiled)
5	chicory leaves
1	Jersey plum tomato
1	lemon

mixed leaves
balsamic vinaigrette dressing
extra virgin olive oil

Method:

1. Sear the chicken breast in a sauté pan with extra virgin olive oil then place in a preheated oven at 185°C for 15 minutes.
2. Boil the egg for 4 minutes and then run it under cold water until the egg is cold.
3. Grill the bacon until crisp, allow to cool and chop into bite size pieces.
4. Slice the tomato and season with a little salt and pepper.
5. Arrange the chicory leaves around a large plate or bowl, toss the mixed leaves in the balsamic dressing and place in the middle of the plate.
6. Place the sliced tomatoes around the lettuce, chop the avocado into chunks and add a little lemon juice, to stop the avocado going brown, then sprinkle around the salad.
7. Slice the chicken and lay on top of the leaves, sprinkle on the crispy bacon and then the crumbled blue cheese.
8. Top the salad with the boiled egg cut into quarters.

balsamic dressing

Ingredients:

4 tbsp extra virgin olive oil
1 tbsp balsamic vinegar
1   clove garlic (crushed)
3 tbsp fresh basil (chopped)
salt and pepper

Method:

Put all the ingredients in a screw top jar and shake and the dressing is ready to go!

Suggested drink:

Rock Shandy (½ lemonade, ½ soda water and a dash of Angostura bitters, slice of lime with lots of ice), or a glass of PG Rosé! We hate the term, but people are using it.

Illustration using
Jersey Pottery Mediterranean range

81

jersey crab and saffron aioli

Cooking crabs:

Choose a saucepan that will easily fit the crab or crabs, half fill the pan with water and heavily salt the water. The water should be salty as this closely resembles the saltiness of the sea water.

Start to heat the water over a medium heat, in the meantime place your crab in the fridge. This allows the crab to drift away as the water starts to heat up. Place the crabs into the saucepan and rapidly bring the water to the boil. If you place the crabs directly into rapidly boiling water it can shock them and cause them to drop their claws. Neither way is a good outcome for the crab but the first way is more humane and you will get a better result.

Once the water returns to the boil, turn it down to a simmer for a few minutes.

We usually work out the cooking time to be 8-10 minutes for 2-3 crabs and a few more minutes if there are more in the pan. The recommended timing is 10 minutes per kg, then we like to leave the crabs in the water for 5 minutes or so, then we drain them straight away.

We do not recommend adding any additional ingredients to the water, such as wine, vinegar or herbs, as we think that the heavily salted water is sufficient and doesn't interfere with the delicate flavour of the crab. The crab can be served cracked of dressed.

Try this dish with some Jersey Royals cooked with a sprig of mint and a mixed salad.

saffron aioli

Ingredients:

30   threads saffron or a good pinch of saffron powder
75ml   dry white wine
3   cloves garlic (peeled and sliced)
250ml   mayonnaise, good quality
2 tsp   lemon juice
salt and pepper

Method:

1. Place the saffron, white wine and garlic into a saucepan and reduce until liquid has almost completely evaporated.
2. Add the lemon juice and allow to cool.
3. Mix into the mayonnaise, check the seasoning and add a little salt and pepper if required.
4. Blend in a food processor.

Suggested wine:

Sancerre Rose, Domaine de Pre Semele – summer in a glass! With picked crab we think it's the best.

83

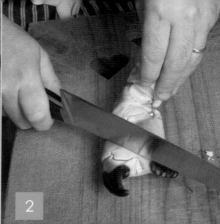

1. The cooked crab ready for action.

2. Remove claws and crack them with the back of a large chopping knife. This allows you to pick the crab meat away.

3. Remove the body of the crab from the back by levering it with your two thumbs.

masterclass: how to dress a crab

4. The back and body separated.

5. Remove dead man's fingers.

6. Dead man's fingers completely removed.

7. Cut the body in half ready to pick.
8. Using a crab pick, carefully pick out the white meat from the body.
9. Break shell away.
10. Flake crab meat out of the claws.
11. Place the white crab meat into carefully cleaned crab shell.

We also sell our crabs in the shell just lightly cooked for our customers to pick themselves if they wish.

jersey style seafood salad with garlic and olive oil and lemon yoghurt

Serves 4 as a main course

Ingredients:

150g	cleaned monkfish (sliced into small pieces)
150g	cleaned squid (cut into rings)
200g	mussels in the shell
80g	cooked picked crab
1	450g lobster
100g	brill fillet (sliced into small pieces)
2	spring onions (sliced)
90ml	olive oil
75ml	white wine
1 tsp	lemon juice
½	fennel head (shredded as finely as possible)
3	shallots (sliced)
1	clove garlic
3 tbsp	chopped parsley
2	handfuls of your favourite salad leaves

Method:

1. Lightly brush 2 baking trays with olive oil. Place the monkfish on one, and the brill on the other. Splash with white wine and put a sheet of silicone paper on each. Place them in the oven at 190°C for 8-10 minutes. The monkfish usually takes more than the brill until it is just cooked. Set the fish aside and allow to cool.
2. Prepare the mussels by pulling the beard away ensuring the mussels are firmly closed. Rinse well in running water for a few minutes and drain well. Throw away any that are broken.
3. Heat a saucepan over a moderate to hot heat and add 1 tablespoon of olive oil, the garlic and the shallots then throw in the mussels straight away. Shake them around the pan then add the white wine and cover with a lid shaking all the time.
4. When all the mussels are open remove them from the heat and add the chopped parsley.
5. To cook the lobster, bring a saucepan of well salted water to a rolling boil. It is best to rest the lobster in the freezer for an hour before to allow the lobster to slip away into a sleep.
6. Drop the lobster into the boiling water and immediately reduce the heat to a simmer. Simmer the lobster for 12-14 minutes (for medium size lobster), then remove and allow to cool for a few minutes before cutting into them.
7. To cook the crab, see page 82 (or you can buy the crab already cooked).
8. Mix the shallots with the spring onions, the teaspoon of lemon juice, the chopped garlic, chopped parsley and remaining olive oil. In a separate bowl mix the picked crab and half of the lemon yoghurt – set aside.
9. Pick the mussels out of the shell, leaving a few in the shell if you desire them for a garnish.
10. Heat a griddle pan over a moderate heat, mix a little olive oil with the squid and season with salt and pepper. Cook on a griddle pan over a high heat, flipping over occasionally for about 90 seconds in total.
11. Mix the mussels and squid with ¾ of shallot dressing, brill and monkfish and season with salt and pepper.

lemon yoghurt

Ingredients:

2 tbsp	mayonnaise
6 tbsp	yoghurt
2 tbsp	chervil and dill (chopped)
	salt and pepper
	zest and juice of
1	lemon

Method:

Mix everything together.

To serve:

Remove the lobster from the shell and divide between four plates. Place a spoon of crab next to it and spoon the seafood mixture around the plate. Mix the fennel and salad together and mix the remainder of the dressing. Spoon a little of the yoghurt dressing onto the centre of the plate and place a little salad on top, or serve the salad separately.

oyster box plateau fruits de mer

When reading other books about 'Fruits de Mer' as well as going to other restaurants in Jersey, Northern France and the UK to sample platters of shellfish, we have found many different interpretations of this dish.

The French eat as much as possible raw, and make up the platter from their own regions. Many places, including us, serve far less of the small shells such as cockles, whelks, clams etc.

A typical plateau fruits de mer at the Oyster Box will consist of:

Half a lobster
Half a Chancre or brown crab
Grilled squid
A few raw oysters
Cooked mussels
Cooked cockles
Cooked clams
1or 2 langoustines per person or king prawns as an alternative and possibly a few cooked prawns

We serve plateau fruits de mer with wedges of lemon, parsley broth, mayonnaise, Marie Rose, shallot vinegar for the oysters and a bottle of tabasco sauce. We have a range of other sauces that we serve with shellfish and you can find the recipes on pages 200 to 203. We also serve a seasonal herb salad and a bowl of buttered Jersey Royals when in season.

Suggested wine:

Many years ago Muscadet was the obvious choice until the new world challenged its dominance, we are now back with Muscadet drinking the wonderful Château de la Cassemichére.

hand dived jersey scallops with garlic herb butter, crisp smoked pancetta and rocket salad

Serves 4

We only use hand dived scallops as they are much more environmentally friendly to catch. Trawling for scallops is like ploughing the sea bed and crushes the infant scallops and other shellfish. Hand dived scallops are also better eating as they have much less chance of containing grit or sand.

Ingredients:

20	hand dived scallops (roe and mussel removed)
10	slices smoked pancetta
2 tbsp	light olive oil for cooking
3 tbsp	chopped parsley
1 tbsp	chopped garlic
100g	Jersey unsalted butter (softened)
1 tbsp	lemon juice
50ml	white wine
3 tbsp	olive oil (good quality)
2	handfuls of rocket
salt and pepper	

Method:

1. Lay the pancetta on a lightly oiled baking tray and place in a preheated oven, 190°C, for 5 minutes until just crisping up. Drain on a kitchen towel to remove the excess grease.
2. In a bowl, mix the butter, parsley, and garlic and season with the salt and pepper. Harden the mixture in the refrigerator and then dice into small pieces.
3. Heat a frying pan to a moderate heat and add a little olive oil, then start adding the scallops in the shape of a clock face. When you get back to the first one it should be ready to turn over. Add a small piece of the garlic butter and shake the pan for a few seconds, then drain the scallops on a kitchen towel.
4. For the dressing, mix the lemon juice and olive oil with a little salt and pepper until combined, then drizzle it over the rocket. Place a little dressed rocket on each of the four plates.
5. Heat a small saucepan over a moderate heat then add the white wine. Let it boil until almost evaporated then whisk in the garlic butter, removing it from the heat when it is al melted. Season to taste.
6. Pour a little of the sauce around the rocket on each plate and arrange the scallops on top of the garlic butter going around the plate. Break each of the pieces of pancetta in half and place a piece on each of the scallops.

Suggested wine:

A young, crisp Chablis.

hand dived jersey scallops with butternut squash and crab risotto

risotto

Ingredients:

600ml	chicken stock (approx)
35g	Jersey butter
1	Small onion (finely chopped)
200g	risotto rice (we prefer carnoroli for this recipe)
50ml	white wine
2 tbsp	chopped parsley
120g	picked crab meat
150g	butternut squash flesh (diced small)
1 tbsp	olive oil
salt and pepper to season	

To serve:

1 tbsp	olive oil
20g	cold Jersey unsalted butter (diced)
30g	parmesan (grated)
12	scallops, roe removed (a good fishmonger will do this for you)
a few rocket leaves	
salt and pepper	

rocket dressing

Ingredients:

1	handful rocket leaves
1	handful basil leaves
1 tbsp	lemon juice
8 tbsp	olive oil
2 tbsp	grated parmesan
salt and pepper	

Suggested wine:

Montagny 1er Cru, Les Vignes de la Croix.

Method:

1. In a frying pan heat the olive oil over a moderate heat, then add the butternut squash and season with salt and pepper. Stir fry for a few minutes until the butternut squash is tender but still firm. Lay on a tray and allow to cool.
2. Heat the chicken stock and leave on a low heat in a thick bottomed pan. Melt 25g of butter on a medium heat in a saucepan and cook the onions in the butter until translucent.
3. Add the rice and stir well keeping on the medium heat for 1 minute.
4. Increase the heat and add the wine, stirring it in until the wine has completely evaporated.
5. Once the wine has evaporated, slowly add the stock a little at a time, ensuring that the rice has absorbed the liquid before adding more.
6. Reduce the heat back to medium and keep adding the liquid until the rice is almost cooked. This will take approximately 18 minutes.
7. Once the rice is nearly cooked add the crab and butternut squash, adding a little more stock if need be.
8. Heat through for about 1 minute then remove from the heat and beat in the parmesan, cold butter and parsley. Adjust the seasoning and it is ready to serve.

Method:

Put all the ingredients in a blender, blend and refrigerate until required.

To serve:

1. Heat a frying pan over a moderate heat, add 1 tablespoon of olive oil, season the scallops with salt and pepper then place them in the pan one by one. Place them in the pan around the edge, cooking each for 1 minute on the first side and 20 seconds on the other. Add the 10g of butter at the end and roll the scallops around the pan coating them in the butter and oil.
2. Drain the scallops on a kitchen towel, divide the risotto between 4 bowls, and place 3 scallops on the top of each risotto.
3. Sprinkle a few rocket leaves over the scallops then drizzle the rocket dressing over the rocket and scallops.

Illustration using
Bespoke ceramic for Oyster Box Jersey

93

bass

Bass, as for all the fish around our shores, is usually caught in good condition. This is due to various factors, including the great tidal flow that brings in fresh water and fresh food such as sand eels. Our close contact with the Jersey fishermen means we can monitor how and where our fish are caught and also means we only purchase wild bass from sustainable, local sources.

The only time we ever purchase bass that is not from local waters is when we have a pre-booked event and the weather goes against us so the local boats can not go out fishing. Most of our bass is line caught, with a few caught on long lines which are checked by the fishermen on an hourly basis.

The bass are at their best and most plentiful in the summer having gone to spawn in the winter months. During this spawning period they are not easy to reach and are in poorer condition. Also, when they are spawning, it is not the best interest of future stocks to take too many of the fish. During the summer and autumn months the fish are at their fittest, as it is necessary for them to fight for their food, and therefore this is when they are at their best to eat, right up until December.

The way in which the fish are caught and stored is very important to us, we find that fish caught in nets are substandard because the fish can often be damaged.

It's important to keep the fish cool and if you are going to keep the fish for a few days, wash it and wrap it in cling film every day; this will keep the freshness for quite a few extra days.

fillet of jersey bass with sweet peppers, grilled squid and lemon dressing

Serves 4

Chef's note on olive oil:

There are many olive oils on the market, however, we find that we like to use different oils for different things. We buy a very neutral French extra virgin olive oil for the bass recipe because it has a very subtle but fruity flavour and blends well with the lemon. The oil also allows the freshness of the fish and the sweetness of the peppers to balance together. There are some heavier olive oils from Italy and Greece that will make hearty dressings to go with pasta dishes or with stronger cheeses and salads.

We tend to have a lot of different oils in our kitchen but you can look around the delis and supermarkets and find the one that you like the taste of most. So much of food is about your personal likes and dislikes: there is not one correct produce or way to prepare a dish.

Ingredients:

4	fillets of bass (175g each, pin bones removed and scored on the skin (any good fishmonger will do this for you)
3 tbsp	light olive oil (for cooking)
2	large red capsicums
1	large yellow capsicum
2 tbsp	lemon juice and the zest of ¼ lemon
6 tbsp	olive oil, good quality (we use La Blanc)
4	pieces of cleaned squid (60g each, scored)
3 tbsp	chopped flat leaf parsley
1	garlic clove (crushed)
20g	Jersey unsalted butter
salt and pepper	

Method:

1. Preheat the oven to 210°C.
2. Cut the capsicums into quarters, remove the seeds and place on a baking tray. Brush the skins with a little of the cooking oil, season with salt and pepper.
3. Place in the oven and cook for approximately 10 minutes until the skins start to blacken but the peppers remain firm. Put them into a bowl and cover them with cling film allowing them to steam slightly for 5 minutes. This will help them to peel more easily.
4. Peel the peppers ensuring you keep the flesh together. If the peppers won't peel easily then they may not be cooked enough. Set the peppers aside to make the dressing.
5. Mix the zest and juice of the lemon and whisk the good quality olive oil into it.
6. Heat up 2 non stick frying pans to a moderate to hot heat, add a little cooking olive oil to one of the pans and place the bass skin side down, seasoned with salt and pepper. Move the fillets around by shaking the pan: this will stop the fillets from sticking. Lower the heat.
7. Fillets of medium thickness will need about 4-5 minutes on the skin side. Half way through, add the butter and, whilst the bass is cooking keep basting the butter over the fish. The fish needs to be cooked mainly on the skin side. This will protect the flesh and stop it from drying out.
8. Meanwhile, in the other pan, season the squid with salt and pepper and place scored side down in the frying pan with a little of the cooking oil for 30-40 seconds. Make sure the pan is very hot.
9. Add the pieces of capsicum and the chopped garlic and move the pan around as the squid starts to curl up. Add a tablespoon of the dressing, the chopped parsley, and then divide the squid and the pepper mixture between four plates.
10. Turn the bass over and finish it for 30 seconds only on the flesh side.
11. Place the bass on top of the squid and pepper mix and spoon the remaining dressing over to serve.

Suggested wine:

Chablis, White Burgundy or Pomino Bianco, Marchesi di Frescobaldi.

dover sole and hand dived jersey scallops with orange and rosemary scented squash

Serves 4 – very healthy portions

Ingredients:

8	fillets of Dover sole (60g each)
12	small scallops
250g	butternut squash (diced)
5 tbsp	olive oil
1 tsp	orange juice and ½ the zest
juice of ½ lemon	
1 tsp	rosemary (chopped)
1 tsp	small capers
20g	unsalted Jersey butter
1 tbsp	flat parsley (chopped)
pinch sugar	
salt and pepper for fish	
pinch salt	

Method:

1. Heat a medium frying pan, add 2 tablespoons of olive oil and then add the butternut squash over a moderate heat. Fry the butternut squash for 6 minutes or so turning regularly until the butternut squash starts to colour, add a pinch of salt and sugar half way through cooking, the butternut squash should still be a little firm.
2. Pull the pan to the side, away from the heat; add the juice and zest of the orange and rosemary.
3. Heat a large non stick frying pan, with 1 more tablespoon of the olive oil. Place the seasoned Dover sole fillets presentation side down, and cook for 2 minutes over a moderate heat on one side then add the scallops and the butter. Turn the sole over then turn the scallops, add the capers, parsley and lemon juice.

To serve:

Place two fillets of the sole and three scallops on each plate and pour a little of the caper butter over them. Spoon some butternut squash onto each plate and a little of its cooking liquid.

Suggested Wine:

Dry white such as Pinot Blanc from Alsace.

Season: Best Autumn / Winter / All Year Round

whole jersey bass baked in a salt crust

Ingredients:

1.2kg bass (scaled)
1 clove of garlic (roughly chopped)
2 tbsp olive oil
6 egg whites (whisked)
350g coarse salt
75g plain flour
1 lemon
1 small bunch of parsley (roughly chopped, save the stalks)
1 stem of rosemary
freshly ground black pepper

Suggested wine:

Exquisite floral qualities in the 'Baron de L' Pouilly Fumé will make the bass come alive. Simply the best Pouilly Fumé to accompany the best line-caught fish.

Method:

1. Preheat oven to 190°C.
2. Scale and trim the fins off the bass and remove the head if you wish.
3. Score the bass three times on each side.
4. Mix the garlic, half the parsley and olive oil together and put to one side.
5. Cut half of the lemon into slices and mix with the parsley stalks and rosemary, and place into the cavity of the bass.
6. Season the bass inside and out with freshly ground pepper the cover the fish with the garlic and parsley mixture.
7. Whisk the egg whites to a firm peak and mix in the flour and course salt and the rest of the parsley.
8. Place a piece of baking parchment on a baking sheet and spread a third of the egg white mix over it using the fish as a template on where to spread it.
9. Place the bass on top of the mix and spoon the rest of the mix over it.
10. Place in the oven and bake for 30 to 35 minutes.
11. Once out of the oven cut around the salt crust and cut away from the fish.
12. Finish by drizzling olive oil over the fish and squeezing the rest of the lemon juice into it. Serve with salad and Jersey Royals when in season.

Chef's tip:

There are a number of sauces that also complement this dish, the warm lemon butter (see page 200) and the ginger sauce (see page 203) would both make superb accompaniments.

100

Season: Winter / Spring

grilled red mullet with saffron risotto and warm tomato dressing

Caught off the east coast of the island by local fishermen.

Ingredients:

4	175g red mullet fillets (scaled and boned)
1 tbsp	olive oil
600ml	chicken stock (see page 202 for recipe)
30g	butter
1	small onion (chopped)
300g	risotto rice
75ml	white wine
20	strands saffron (a good pinch)
50g	cold unsalted Jersey butter (diced)
50g	grated parmesan

salt and pepper

warm tomato dressing

Ingredients:

75ml	basic tomato sauce (see page 72)
1 tbsp	balsamic vinegar
2 tbsp	olive oil
2	plum tomatoes (de-seeded and diced)

a few basil leaves (chopped)

Method:

1. Heat the chicken stock and leave on a low heat in a heavy based pan.
2. Melt 30g of butter on a medium heat in a saucepan and cook the onions in the butter until translucent.
3. Add the rice and stir well keeping on the medium heat for 1 minute.
4. Increase the heat and add the wine and the saffron, stirring it in until the wine has completely evaporated. Season with a little salt and pepper.
5. Once the wine has evaporated, slowly add the stock, ensuring that the rice has absorbed the liquid before adding more.
6. Reduce the heat back to medium and keep adding the liquid until the rice is almost cooked. This will take approximately 18 minutes.
7. Remove from the heat and beat in the parmesan and cold butter. Adjust the seasoning and it is ready to serve.

To make the warm tomato dressing

1. In a small saucepan warm the tomato sauce and stir in the balsamic vinegar. Mix in the olive oil and add the diced tomato. Season with salt and pepper and add in the basil leaves.
2. Leave in a warm place for 10 minutes to let all the flavours infuse.

To cook the fish

1. Brush the skin with olive oil, season with salt and pepper, and lay on a grilling tray.
2. Place under a hot grill for 3-4 minutes until the skin has turned golden and crisp and the heat has just penetrated the flesh. Alternatively, you can pan fry the red mullet, skin side down.
3. Divide the risotto between 4 bowl plates, place the red mullet on top and spoon the warm tomato dressing over them.

Suggested wine:

Cape Mentelle, Semillon, Sauvignon Blanc.

Illustration using
Bespoke ceramics for Oyster Box Jersey

Season: Spring

fillet of john dory with spiced butter sauce and tempura of courgette flower stuffed with wild mushrooms

Ingredients:

4	skinless fillets of John Dory (175g each)
2 tbsp	olive oil
4	courgette flowers

spice mix

Ingredients:

1 tsp	grated ginger
1 tsp	curry powder
1 tsp	cumin
1 tsp	cinnamon
1 tsp	coriander seeds (crushed)

zest of 1 lemon (finely grated)
zest of ½ orange (finely grated)
good pinch saffron

Method for spice mix:

1. Put all the ingredients in a frying pan over a medium heat, apart from the orange and lemon zest.
2. Move the spice mix around regularly to prevent burning, just tossing it gently for 3-4 minutes.
3. Remove from the heat and add the zest to the mix, allow to cool. Crush a little in the pestle and mortar to mix the zest in.

basic butter sauce

Ingredients:

3	shallots (finely chopped)
1	star anise
100ml	dry white wine
30ml	white wine vinegar
75ml	Jersey whipping cream
100g	Jersey unsalted butter (diced)
1 tsp	chopped tarragon
salt and pepper	
juice of ½ lemon	

Method:

1. Put a small piece of butter into a saucepan and melt it, add the chopped shallots and star anise and cook gently over a moderate heat for 3-4 minutes. Increase the heat and add the white wine and white wine vinegar, reduce until the liquid has almost completely evaporated.
2. Add the cream and reduce until the cream starts to thicken, season with salt and pepper then whisk in the butter and finish with the tarragon.
3. When the sauce is ready to serve whisk in 2 teaspoons of the spice mix and a squeeze of lemon juice.

stuffing for courgette flowers

Ingredients:

1	shallot (finely chopped)
1	clove garlic (finely chopped)
100g	mixed wild mushrooms (chopped quite small)
2 tbsp	Madeira (or white wine if you don't have Maderia)
1 sprig	thyme
50ml	whipping cream
2 tbsp	olive oil
½ tsp	light white truffle oil (optional)
salt and pepper	

Suggested wine:

A good, crisp Sauvignon Blanc from South Africa.

Method:

1. In a non stick frying pan heat the olive oil until almost smoking. Add the mushrooms, shallots and garlic and season with salt and pepper. Stir fry for a minute or so then add the Madeira and thyme.
2. Let the Madeira completely evaporate, add the cream and reduce until thick and glossy. Remove from the heat and allow to cool. When cool stir in the truffle oil if using.
3. On a table put 4 separate pieces of cling film. Remove the core of each courgette flower and replace with the wild mushroom mix, divided between the four flowers. Be careful not to over fill, then twist the ends of the flowers and wrap them in the cling film. This helps them to retain their shape.
4. Remove the cling film, roll them through seasoned flour, then into tempura batter (see recipe on page 203) and into the deep fat fryer at 175°C for 3-4 minutes.
5. Drain on a kitchen towel and season with salt and pepper.

To cook the fish:

1. Heat a non stick frying pan, add the olive oil then place the seasoned fillets of fish presentation side (the side that was in contact with the bone and not the skin) down and shake the pan as you do, to prevent the fish from sticking.
2. After a minute turn the heat down and add a small piece of butter after 2 more minutes turn the fish over and finish it for 1 more minute. Remove the fish from the pan and set it in a warm place.

To serve:

Place two spoons of the spiced butter on one side of four large plates, then place the fish on top and put the courgette flower next to it.

jersey brill baked in banana leaf served with nam jim dressing and white radish and cucumber salad

Serves 4

This dish could be barbecued over a low burning barbecue and works really well with bass and local black bream.

We discovered Nam Jim dressing through a colleague we worked with a few years ago. He discovered it in Australia when he was travelling the world. It is a fantastic, versatile dressing with a brilliant balance of flavours and gives a fresh, summer feel to a fish dish without overpowering it.

Banana leaves are available in Asian food stores, and also available frozen in some supermarkets.

Ingredients:

4	fillets of Jersey brill (175g each)
4	pieces of banana leaf (cut about 4cm wide)
1 tbsp	vegetable oil

Method:

1. Lay out the strips of banana leaf. In a bowl mix your fish fillets with the vegetable oil and 3 tablespoons of the Nam Jim and 2 or 3 grinds of a peppermill.
2. Lay the fish on the banana leaf and wrap them up into a parcel.
3. Place on a lightly oiled baking tray and put in a preheated oven 190°C for 10 minutes.

nam jm dressing

Ingredients:

4	cloves of garlic (sliced)
½	large bunch of coriander (including stalks)
1 tsp	Maldon (or other coarse) salt
2	long red chillies
2	long green chillies
2 tbsp	palm sugar
40ml	fish sauce
80ml	fresh lime juice
4	shallots (sliced)

Method:

1. Pound the garlic, coriander, salt, chillies, palm sugar and shallots down, either with a pestle and mortar or a food processor.
2. Mix in the fish sauce and lime juice.

white radish and cucumber salad

Ingredients:

½	cucumber
½	white radish (moulli)

Method:

1. Peel the cucumber and the radish and cut them into long thin strips, discarding the cucumber seed.
2. Mix through a dressing of your choice, such as a little lemon and olive oil, or our personal favourite, soy salad dressing (on page 200)

To serve:

Place the brill on a plate, cut the top of the banana leaf so it springs open and serve with a pot of Nam Jim dressing and the radish and cucumber salad.

Illustration using
Jersey Pottery Cook and Serve Fruits de Mer range

107

fillet of turbot with coriander, ginger and lentil sauce

Serves 4

Turbot, along with bass and Dover sole are among our favourite fish in the sea and we do get plenty of turbot in local waters at certain times of year, particularly in April and May. We also have a turbot farm in Jersey but you can't beat the great 3-5kg size fish caught offshore with fantastic, firm flesh.

You really don't need to do much to turbot – poach, grill or pan fry it and serve it with nutty butter or hollandaise sauce. Turbot also makes fantastic fish and chips, fried in our tempura batter (see recipe on page 203), but it may be a bit extravagant as turbot is not the cheapest of fish.

Ingredients:

4	pieces turbot fillet (175g each, skin removed)
4 tbsp	olive oil
100ml	vermouth
75ml	white wine
150g	shallots (sliced)
30g	ginger (grated)
1	clove garlic (crushed)
300ml	chicken stock
100ml	double cream
50g	diced Jersey butter
½ tsp	ground coriander
3 tbsp	fresh coriander (chopped)
60g	red lentils (soaked for 1 hour, then drained)
1 tsp	lemon juice
120g	mixed wild mushrooms

Method:

1. In a saucepan heat one tablespoon of the olive oil over a moderate heat, add the shallots and garlic and cook for 2-3 minutes without colour.
2. Add the ginger and the ground coriander and season with salt and pepper. Cook for 2 more minutes then add the white wine and vermouth, increase the heat and reduce until the liquid has almost evaporated. Add the red lentils and chicken stock and simmer until the lentils are cooked.
3. Add the cream, bring back to the boil then put into a liquidiser and blend. Add the lemon juice, butter and finally the fresh coriander. If it is a little thick, add a little more chicken stock at this stage.
4. To cook the fish, heat a non stick frying pan and add 2 tablespoons of the olive oil. Heat until almost smoking and then place the pieces of seasoned turbot presentation side down. Presentation side is the side that was in contact with the bone and not the skin.
5. Reduce the heat and add a small piece of the butter, shaking the fish around to stop it sticking. Lower the heat even more, to very low, and cook for about 3-4 minutes in total. Flip it over and cook for a further minute. Remove from the pan.
6. Pour sauce divided evenly onto 4 plates then place a piece of fish on top of each of the plates.
7. At the last minute heat a frying pan until almost smoking. Add the rest of the olive oil and sauté the wild mushrooms. Season with salt and pepper and sprinkle over the turbot.

Suggested wine:

We would certainly go for anything Chardonnay based, but would also love to have our Chablis 1er Cru, from Jean Durup.

fillet of smoked haddock with leek and potato broth

Serves 4

Ingredients:

4	portions natural smoked haddock (approx 175g each, skin on)
300ml	Jersey milk
50g	Jersey unsalted butter
4	free range eggs
2 tbsp	white wine vinegar
2 tbsp	olive oil
100g	leeks (finely diced)
100g	Spanish onion (finely diced)
200g	potatoes (peeled and finely diced)
100g	fennel (finely diced)
500ml	chicken stock (see page 202 for recipe)
50ml	Jersey whipping cream
2	cloves garlic (crushed)
1	bay leaf

Method:

1. Heat a heavy based saucepan, add the olive oil, onion and garlic and cook for 3-4 minutes on a low heat.
2. Add the leeks and fennel, season with salt and pepper, and cook for a further 2-3 minutes.
3. Add the potatoes, bay leaf and chicken stock, bring to the boil and simmer for 20 minutes until the potatoes are cooked. Set the pan aside.
4. Brush a deep baking tray with half the butter and lay the fillets of smoked haddock skin side up, pour on the milk, using just enough to cover the fish, and cover with silicone paper. Place in a preheated oven at 190°C for 7-8 minutes.
5. To poach the eggs fill a saucepan half full with water, add the vinegar and a good pinch of salt. Lower the heat to a simmer and start moving the water with a perforated spoon so the water moves as you add the eggs.
6. Crack the eggs into the moving water; the moving water helps the eggs to stay together.
7. The eggs will take approximately 2 ½ minutes on a simmer, then drain them on a kitchen towel.
8. To serve, bring the broth to a boil, finish it with the cream and the remaining butter and dish it onto a bowl. Remove the smoked haddock skin and lay the fish in the broth. Place the egg on top of the smoked haddock, spooning a little melted butter with a little chopped parsley over the egg if desired.

Suggested wine:

Chardonnay, Ardéche, Louis Latour – Matthew's favourite white wine.

Season: Autumn / Winter

smoked fish and shellfish pie with potato and jersey cheddar

Serves 4 – can be made into individual dishes or as one large dish.

Ingredients:

200g	natural smoked haddock (diced)
150g	salmon (or mackerel) fillet (diced)
4	raw king prawns (each one cut into 3)
150g	John Dory fillet (or other firm white fish)
4	scallops (each one cut into 3)
250ml	Jersey double cream
1 tsp	English mustard
3 tbsp	parmesan, grated
100g	shallots, sliced
2 tbsp	parsley, chopped
175ml	white wine
1	clove garlic
300ml	Jersey milk
50g	Jersey butter
30g	flour
5	medium potatoes for mashing
75g	mature Jersey cheddar (grated)
1 tbsp	olive oil

Suggested wine:

Sauvignon Blanc would be a good choice with this dish; our Fish Hoek Sauvignon Blanc is quite scrummy!

Method:

1. Brush a baking tray with olive oil, lay the smoked haddock on the tray and cover with 250ml of the milk. Cover with parchment paper and place in a preheated oven at 190°C for 8 minutes. Carefully remove the fish from the milk and allow to cool.
2. On a separate baking tray repeat this process with the other fish, apart from the scallops, season with salt and pepper, this time covering the fish using 100ml of the white wine. Cover with parchment paper again and place in a preheated oven at 190°C for 7 minutes, again removing the fish from the trays at the end of cooking and allowing to cool.
3. Reserve the cooking liquid.
4. In a saucepan add 30g of the butter and melt over a moderate heat. Add the shallots and garlic and cook over a gentle heat for 5 minutes without much colour. Add the flour and cook for 2 minutes then add the remaining white wine and the cooking liquid from the fresh fish. Reduce, stirring all the time then slowly start adding the strained milk from cooking the haddock. When it has completely evaporated add 200ml of the cream and cook over a gentle heat for 15-20 minutes, stirring regularly. Remove from the heat, stir in the mustard and the parmesan and allow to cool.
5. To make the mashed potato, peel the potatoes and chop them into medium sized pieces. Place them in a saucepan, just cover with water and add a good teaspoon or two of salt to taste. Bring to the boil then simmer until cooked (about 25 minutes).
6. Drain the potatoes in a colander and place the remaining 20g of butter, 50ml milk and 50ml cream in the saucepan and gently heat.
7. Put the potatoes through a masher then mix them into the milk mixture, check the seasoning and allow them to cool slightly.
8. When the fish has cooled, evenly split the fish into 4 individual pie dishes or place into 1 large dish. Mix the parsley into the sauce then pour the sauce over the fish evenly. Allow to set in the fridge for ½ hour then spread (or pipe in a piping bag) the potato over the pies and sprinkle with cheddar cheese.
9. Place on a baking tray and bake for 20 minutes at 190°C for individual dishes, or 30 minutes for a large dish.
10. Serve with green vegetables.

Illustration using
Jersey Pottery Cook and Serve Fruits de Mer range

jersey style fish stew with saffron mashed potato

This is our version of the classic provincial fish dish 'Bouillabaisse' with a few twists. Having spent some time cooking in Provence many years ago, Tony won't even try to call his fish stew a Bouillabaisse. In Provence families feud over who has made their Bouillabasse correctly with the right fish, the right ingredients in the soup and the correct accompaniments. Quite similar to how an Irishman views his stew, a Scotsman his haggis or a Jerseyman his bean crock!

   We have used a combination of methods, mixing the way the dish is made in the South of France, with an Italian twist, and varied it to reflect the ingredients and fish available here in Jersey. The dish could be served with the fiery chilli dip called Rouille, but we try to use the same ingredients and accompaniments as in the French recipes, and spread these throughout the recipe.

Ingredients:

700g	mixed fish (boned weight; so when buying whole fish double it)
1	small onion (sliced)
1	stick of celery (sliced)
½	leek (sliced)
2	garlic cloves
1 tbsp	olive oil
1	bay leaf
1	glass white wine
peppercorns	

Method:

1. Fillet the fish; remove the pin bones, retaining all of the bones. Cut the fish into even size chunks.
   Slice the squid into rings and clean and wash the mussels. Make sure that the bass, mullet and gurnard is scaled but not skinned (the fishmonger can do this for you).
2. In a saucepan heat the olive oil and add the vegetables, fish bones, bay leaf, a few peppercorns and a glass of white wine and cook for a minute or so.
3. Add 1 litre of water and bring to the boil. Simmer for a further 25 minutes before passing it through a fine strainer.

to make the sauce base

Ingredients:

1	small onion (chopped)
1	stick of celery (peeled and chopped)
2	cloves of garlic (finely chopped)
½ tsp	ginger (grated)
3 tbsp	olive oil
1 dstsp	tomato puree
1	bay leaf
1	good pinch saffron
1	dried chilli (crushed)
1 tsp	curry powder
50ml	Ricard
50ml	white wine
300ml	fish stock
1	tin of chopped tomatoes (400g)
4 tbsp	chopped parsley

juice of ½ a lemon
salt and pepper

Method:

1. In a wide heavy based sauce pan (a very wide thick base Le Creuset dish would be perfect) heat the olive oil to a moderate heat, add the onions and the celery and cook for 2-3 minutes, without too much colour. Add the garlic, ginger, bay leaf, saffron, chilli and curry powder and cook for 3 more minutes stirring regularly. Season with salt and pepper.
2. Add the tomato puree and cook for a further minute, add the white wine and Ricard and boil vigorously. Increase the heat for a minute or so, boiling the alcohol away, and then add the tinned tomato and the fish stock.
3. Reduce the heat and simmer for about an hour and the sauce should start to thicken.
4. Bring the sauce back to the boil and then start to add the seasoned fish.
5. Start with the monkfish spreading it around the dish, then after a minute reduce the heat and add the other fish, leaving out the squid and the mussels.
6. After about 4 minutes, add the squid and the mussels. Cover with a lid, giving the dish a further 3-4 minutes.
7. Squeeze over the lemon juice, sprinkle with parsley, the dish is ready to be served.

saffron mash

Ingredients:

800g	waxy potatoes (cut into even sized pieces)
2 tbsp	salt, plus more to taste
100g	Jersey unsalted butter
125ml	milk
40g	grated parmesan

good pinch of saffron (about 15 strands)
pepper

Suggested wine:

Bandol Rosé from Provence or, if you want to push the boat out, Domaine Ott Rosé; expensive but worth it.

Method:

1. Place the potatoes in a saucepan, fill up with water, about 2 inches above the potatoes, add saffron and salt.
2. Bring to the boil and then simmer for about 20 minutes so the potatoes are just cooked. Drain them in a colander then put them through a potato ricer or mash them with a home-style potato masher.
3. Put the mash back onto the heat and gradually beat in the butter and the milk. This potato dish is quite wet, so season with more salt if required, then add the ground pepper and the parmesan.

To serve:

Divide the mash between 4 bowl plates on one side and spoon the fish stew onto the other side. Serve with extra grated parmesan if required.

Chef's tip:

We use fresh fish and fish with good skin so it holds the fish together, such as gurnard, bass, red mullet, squid and mussels.

barbecuing principles

The best thing to use to cook fish on a barbecue is a folding grill, as used in our bream recipe opposite. If you do not have one of these the fish will need to wrapped in something like foil or baking parchment to protect it. There are a few exceptions to this, fish such as monkfish, squid, king prawns and scallops are firm enough to be put straight onto the barbecue grill without the fish breaking up.

It is best not to marinade things like king prawns and scallops in oils or marinades before cooking. If you do this the oil will flame and the fish will not cook evenly. What we find works best is to season the fish before placing on the hot grill then halfway through cooking brush the fish with a flavoured oil or marinade.

tips on barbecuing

We do many events requiring barbecues in many parts of Jersey, on the beaches, cliff edges, at castles and at Durrel Wildlife Conservation park to name a few.

We use both gas and charcoal barbecues each of them having certain benefits which suit cooking different cuts of meat and fish.

The large gas barbecues are ideal for larger pieces of meat with indirect heat. For example a piece of beef brisket can be cooked slowly by placing it away from the direct heat of the flames and keeping the barbecue on a low heat setting with the lid closed. After 6-8 hours the result will be a succulent and tender piece of meat. Serve this with a tangy barbecue sauce and rocket salad. It doesn't come much better than this.

When cooking fish we tend to prefer the traditional charcoal barbecues.

It is important to allow the charcoal to burn for a while before cooking. Many people make the mistake of putting the food on too soon after lighting and resulting in the food tasting like charcoal and cooking unevenly. As a general rule, let the charcoal burn for at least an hour, the charcoal needs to have turned grey and ash like before cooking. In windy conditions this stage may be reached sooner.

When we are working on the cliffs we make sure there is spare charcoal to hand ready to throw on in case the barbecue burns a bit too quickly.

116

Ingredients:

4   fillets of black bream (175g each, scaled and bones removed)
2   heads fennel
1   small onion (sliced)
1   bay leaf
1   clove garlic (sliced)
300ml chicken stock (see page 202 for recipe)
2 tbsp olive oil
½ tsp   coriander seeds
50ml   white wine
50ml   Ricard (optional)
zest of ½ orange
good sprig rosemary
salt and pepper

Method:

1. Remove the outer layers, the tips and a little of the root from the fennel and cut each one into quarters. Heat the oil in a medium size saucepan then add the fennel, season with salt and pepper and fry over a moderate heat for 2-3 minutes until golden brown.
2. Add the onions and garlic and cook for a further minute. Then add the orange zest, bay leaf, rosemary, coriander seeds, white wine and Ricard (if you decide to use it).
3. Reduce over a high heat until the alcohol has completely evaporated.
4. Add the chicken stock, cover with grease proof paper and foil and place in a preheated oven at 150°C for 1 ¼ hours.
5. This is now ready to finish on the barbecue. If you would like this as a braised dish continue cooking it for a further 15 minutes until the fennel is very soft.

BBQ fillets of jersey black bream with twice cooked fennel and salsa verdi

salsa verdi

Ingredients:

100g	herbs (equal quantities of flat leaf parsley, chervil, basil and mint all pinched away from stalk, and chives finely chopped)
2	cocktail gerkins (roughly chopped)
6 or 7	capers
1 tsp	Dijon mustard
1-2	anchovies (optional)
100ml	olive oil
2	spring onions (finely sliced)

juice of ½ lemon.

Method:

1. Place all ingredients, except the spring onions and lemon juice in a food processor and blend for 20 seconds or so until you have a salsa texture.
2. Mix in the lemon juice and spring onions.

To finish on the barbecue:

1. When the barbecue is ready, season the fish with salt and pepper and place them on the folding grill racks. Place the racks at least 15 inches above the charcoals. Cook for 6 minutes on the first side them turn over and cook for one more minute.
2. While the fish is cooking lay the fennel on the bbq, season with a little salt and pepper. Keep turning the fennel throughout cooking; it should take about the same amount of time as the fish.

To serve:

Arrange two pieces of fennel on each plate and place a piece of bream on top and then spoon some salsa verdi over the fish.

jersey lobster served with raspberry vinaigrette dressed salad and garlic mayonnaise

Serves 4

Ingredients:

2	live Jersey lobsters (750g each)
2 tbsp	olive oil
1	lemon
salt and pepper	

raspberry vinaigrette

Ingredients:

2 tbsp raspberry vinegar
6 tbsp light olive oil
juice ½ lemon

to serve

Ingredients:

salad leaves of your choice, mixed with dandelion leaf and a mix of ripe tomatoes and chives
garlic mayonnaise (recipe, see page 203)

Suggested wine:

Domaine de La Mare from La Mare Wine Estate Jersey or St Aubin 1er Cru.

Method:

1. Put the lobster in the deep freeze for 1 hour allowing the lobster to drift away, and then plunge it into boiling salted water. Work on 40g of salt to 1 litre of water. Reduce the heat and allow the lobsters to simmer for 3-4 minutes, this won't cook them but will start the cooking process.
2. Remove from the water and allow to cool for a few minutes. When the lobsters are just warm, split them straight down the centre, and remove the innards at the top of the head. Lay the two halves on a tray, sprinkle them with a little coarse salt and they are ready to grill.
3. Lay the lobster shell side down on the barbecue for a few minutes, just to allow the heat to start to penetrate the flesh without drying the flesh out. After 3 minutes, turn the lobsters over and cook for a further 3 minutes, brushing them with a little oil nearer the end.
4. Mix the raspberry vinegar, olive oil and lemon juice to make the vinaigrette.

To serve:

Brush the lobster with a little more oil and cut the lemon into wedges, sprinkle the juice on the lobster. Dress the salad with the raspberry vinaigrette and serve in a bowl with a pot of garlic mayonnaise on the side, and some Jersey Royals when in season.

Chef's tip:

When grilling a lobster, never cut through it live and put it straight on the barbecue as we find that this method dries the flesh.

119

sirloin of beef with chilli rub and balsamic salad served with jersey royals

chilli rub

Ingredients:

2 tbsp	sugar
4	cloves garlic (finely chopped)
1 tbsp	dry chilli (crushed)
1 tbsp	salt
1 tbsp	Schezuan pepper
100ml	olive oil

Method:
1. Combine all the ingredients together.
2. Marinate 1kg of trimmed sirloin of beef in the rub for 12-24 hours.

Salad

Ingredients:

3	handfuls rocket leaves
50g	parmesan shavings
1 tbsp	good quality balsamic vinegar
3 tbsp	olive oil

Method:
1. Preheat a griddle pan or barbecue over a moderate heat, brush off the excess marinade.
2. Place the meat on the griddle pan and keep turning until it has a good colour. Seal it for 8 minutes then place it in a preheated oven at 180°C for 10-15 minutes depending on how you would like it cooked. Allow to rest for 5 minutes or so.
3. Slice the beef.
4. Mix all the salad ingredients together and serve in a bowl next to the sliced beef.
5. Serve with chips, sauté potatoes or Jersey Royals when in season.

Suggested wine:

Red Rioja or a big, flavoursome white.

Illustration using
Jersey Pottery Jersey Royal Bowl

121

jersey fish with fragrant green curry sauce

Ingredients:

100g	shallots (sliced)
1	long green chilli (sliced)
1	clove garlic (sliced)
½ tsp	grated ginger
1 tsp	palm sugar
½ tsp	green curry paste
¼ stick	lemon grass (sliced)
300ml	chicken stock
300ml	coconut milk
1	lime leaf
1 handful	basil leaves
2 handfuls	coriander leaves
1 tbsp	fish sauce
1 tbsp	vegetable oil

mixed fish (175g per person)
zest and juice of 1 lime
salt

To grill:

8 sticks	lemon grass

Suggested drink:

Serve with a cold beer or dry Gewürztraminer.

Method:

1. Heat the vegetable oil in a medium saucepan, add the shallots, garlic and ginger and cook over a moderate heat for 2 minutes without too much colour. Add the chilli, lime leaves and lemon grass and cook for a further minute.
2. Add the curry paste and chicken stock, bring to the boil and reduce the chicken stock by half. Add the coconut milk, bring to the boil and simmer for 5 minutes.
3. Add the fish sauce, lime juice and zest. Add the palm sugar then add the coriander and basil and liquidise for 1 minute until the herbs are completely incorporated. Add a little salt if required.
4. To grill your fish you need a selection of fish you like. We use red mullet, John Dory, monkfish and mackerel – all firm, delicate fish that stand up to the power of the curry.
5. You will need 1 bunch of lemon grass lightly bashed up, light your barbecue and let the charcoals become completely white. Spread the lemon grass on the barbecue and place your small pieces of fish on top of the lemon grass. This will give you a great flavour and protect the fish from sticking to the barbecue.
6. Allow the fish to cook for about 3-4 minutes turning half way through allowing the flavours of the lemon grass to come through.

To serve:

Pour the sauce into a bowl, disburse the fish on top. Sprinkle with coriander and serve with jasmine rice.

Chef's tip:

This dish is also nice served with some strips of green mango and green chilli sprinkled over it. This will add extra sourness and heat to the dish.

barbecued poussin with lemon paprika and cumin

Ingredients:

4	poussin (ask your butcher to remove the back bone to achieve what is known as spatchcock)

for the marinade:

100g	coriander
1	clove garlic (chopped)
1 tbsp	paprika
1 tsp	ground cumin
1 tbsp	lemon juice
½ tsp	chilli powder (optional – gives the dish a kick)
2 tbsp	olive oil

Method:

1. Mix all the ingredients together and pour over the poussins. Cover and leave in the fridge to marinade for at least 12 hours preferably 24 hours.
2. Heat the BBQ for approximately 10 minutes, on a medium setting.
3. Season the poussins with salt and pepper and place on the racks of the barbecue that are away from the flames. (If you have three 'flame bars' on your barbecue only light two of them and place the poussins over the one that is not lit).
4. Keep the lid shut and cook for about half an hour. Check they are cooked then turn off the heat and allow them to rest for 5 minutes.

To serve:

We like to serve this barbecue dish on a hot summer's day with a citrus salad like the crispy fried duck salad on page 128.

Chef's tip:

This is best cooked on a gas barbecue with a lid to be able to take advantage of indirect heat.

Suggested wine:

Try a glass or two of chilled Gewurztraminer with this recipe; the spice and citrus flavours go very well together.

124

beef satay skewers with peanut, soy and ginger dip

Serves 5 to 6 canapés each for 4 people
This could be cooked on a barbecue

Ingredients:

500g   fillet of beef (well trimmed and cut into 20 small pieces)
salt and pepper

For the marinade:

2 tbsp pineapple juice
1 tbsp peanut butter
2 tbsp light soy sauce
2 tbsp chilli bean sauce
1   garlic clove (crushed)
salt and pepper

Method:

1. Mix all the ingredients together for the marinade and place the beef in the marinade for at least 3-4 hours, or overnight.
2. Drain the beef from the marinade.
3. Heat a griddle pan or barbecue to a moderate heat.
4. Season the pieces of fillet with salt and pepper and brush them with a little vegetable oil.
5. Turn the heat up until the pan starts to smoke. Carefully start grilling your pieces, turning them every 30 seconds for a total of 2 minutes.
6. Remove from the heat, skewer each piece of beef with a cocktail stick or a fancy canapé skewer.
7. Serve with a pot of peanut, soy and ginger dip (recipe on page 200).

Suggested drink:

Great served with a chilled local beer from Jersey Brewery called *It's Time*, which was launched to celebrate Durrell Wildlife Conservation Trust's 50th birthday. Some of the proceeds of each bottle go towards raising money to help save endangered animals.
www.durrellwildlife.org

crispy fried duck breast with chicory and watercress salad and citrus and soy dressing

Serves 4

Ingredients:

2	fresh duck breasts
2	pink grapefruits
2	oranges
½ tsp	Szechuan pepper
juice of	1 lime
1 tbsp	honey
1 tsp	salt
2 tbsp	light soy sauce
1 tbsp	marjoram (chopped)
1	shallot (finely chopped)
2 tbsp	vegetable oil
1 tbsp	sesame oil
1	bunch of watercress (large, stalks removed and washed)
1	head chicory (shredded, core removed)

Method:

1. Squeeze the juice of one orange and half a grapefruit into a bowl, add the marjoram and mix it with the Szechuan pepper, lime juice, soy sauce, honey, salt, sesame oil and shallots.
2. Pour it over the duck breasts and marinade for 3 hours in the fridge.
3. Remove the duck breasts from the marinade and pour the marinade into a saucepan. To make the dressing, reduce the liquid by half, set aside and when cool whisk in the sesame oil, vegetable oil and add segments from the other orange and grapefruit.
4. Season the duck with a little salt, then heat a frying pan over a moderate heat and place the duck breasts in the pan, skin side down.
5. Lower the heat slightly and cook gently on the skin side only, pouring the fat away as it renders out of the duck. This will take about 7 minutes.
6. Flip the duck breast over and cook for 1 minute on the other side, remove from the pan and rest in a warm place on a plate for 3-4 minutes
7. Mix the chicory and watercress together then divide between four plates. Slice the duck breasts quite thinly, spreading the slices on top of the salad, spoon the dressing over the duck and the salad.

Suggested wine:

An Australian Shiraz.

roast loin of venison with spiced red cabbage and chestnut crumbs

We use venison from the Highlands of Scotland and find that we achieve consistently good quality dishes.

Ingredients:

650-700g	venison loin (off the bone)
150ml	full bodied red wine
25g	Jersey unsalted butter
1 sprig	fresh thyme
1 tbsp	olive oil

Method:

1. Make sure that the venison loin is completely trimmed of sinew, sprinkle with some picked thyme and pour on the red wine. Cover with an air tight lid or cling film and leave in the refrigerator for 12-24 hours then drain.

chestnut crumbs

Ingredients:

3 slices	white breadcrumbs (see chef's tip on page 54)
8	chestnuts (cooked and peeled, we use ready prepared)
½	lemon zest (grated)
2 tbsp	flat parsley
3 tbsp	olive oil
salt and pepper	

Method:

1. In a non stick frying pan, add 2 tablespoon of the olive oil, heat to a moderate heat and add the breadcrumbs. Cook until nice and golden brown – remove from the heat.
2. Put the lemon zest, the rest of the olive oil, and chestnuts into a food processor and pulse until the chestnuts are well broken up but not too powdery. At the last minute mix everything together and season with salt and pepper.

spiced red cabbage

Ingredients:

300g	red cabbage (finely shredded)
1	Granny Smith apple (grated)
1 tsp	orange zest (grated)
½ stick	cinnamon
200ml	red wine
100ml	red wine vinegar
50g	brown sugar
1	clove garlic (crushed)
2	shallots (finely chopped)
1	bay leaf
60g	Jersey butter (diced)
pinch of nutmeg	
salt and pepper	

Method:

1. Put all the ingredients (except the butter) into a fridge container, season with salt and pepper and marinade overnight.
2. Put the cabbage mix into a casserole dish, cover with a lid and place in a preheated oven 150°C for 2 hours. When cooked, beat in the butter and check the seasoning.
3. To cook the venison, preheat the oven to 185°C, heat a frying pan to a moderate heat, add olive oil, season the venison and seal it all over, giving it a nice brown colour. Then place it on a baking tray and top it with the butter. Cook for about 8-10 minutes for a loin of medium thickness. This should cook the meat medium-rare.
4. Remove the meat from the oven and rest it in a warm place for 5 minutes.

Suggested wine:

Left Bank Claret or Haut Brion – Robert's favourite red wine.

To serve:

Divide the cabbage between 4 plates; slice the venison on top of the cabbage and sprinkle the chestnut crumbs over the top. We usually serve this dish with a red wine or Madeira sauce (see recipe on page 201). It is also nice to finish your sauce with a small amount of bitter chocolate, as this goes particularly well with venison.

fillet of pork with white bean and white truffle flavour mash, sauté spinach and madeira sauce

Ingredients:

2	fillets of pork (350g each, trimmed)
50g	dried white haricot beans
1 tsp	thyme leaves (chopped)
½	lemon (zest)
2 tbsp	olive oil
½ tsp	white truffle oil
¾ kg	spinach
30g	Jersey unsalted butter
100ml	hot vegetable stock (see recipe on page 201)
100ml	Madeira sauce (see recipe on page 201)
50ml	Jersey milk
2	grates nutmeg
salt and pepper	

Suggested wine:

Cabernet Sauvignon or any full bodied red.

Method:

1. Soak the haricot beans overnight in plenty of cold water, rinse them and place them in a pan of water. Don't add salt at this stage. Bring to the boil and simmer for 20 minutes or so until the beans are tender.
2. Place the beans into a food processor and blend with the vegetable stock. You can also use the cooking liquid from the beans. Add 10g of butter, 1 tablespoon of olive oil and the milk. Season with salt and pepper and blend, add the white truffle oil, and place in a saucepan ready to warm the mixture through.
3. Pick the big stalks from the spinach and discard, wash thoroughly in a deep sink of cold water. Drain in a colander.
4. Bring a saucepan of salted water to the boil and add the spinach. Cook for 30 seconds then plunge the spinach into a water bath filled with ice. Allow to cool then squeeze the spinach water out with your hands. Roughly slice through the spinach and leave to the side.
5. Season the pork fillet with salt and pepper and rub the lemon zest and thyme over it. Fry in the remaining olive oil until you have a nice colour.
6. Place in a preheated oven at 185°C for approximately 12 minutes, it should be slightly under cooked and will just finish off as you rest it in a warm place for 5 minutes covered with foil.
7. Heat the remaining butter in a saucepan; add the spinach and stir fry it over a moderate heat. Season with salt and pepper and a little nutmeg. Warm the white bean puree through.

To serve:

Spoon a little of the puree onto a plate and place some spinach next to it. Slice the pork on top and spoon the Madeira sauce over the top of the pork.

jersey pottery yorkshire puddings made with beer

Makes 18 puddings

Over the years we have made many Yorkshire puddings to serve with our Sunday roasts. The traditional recipes that require equal amounts of milk, eggs and flour work well and make fantastic Yorkshire puddings. It is imperative that you get the fat in the trays almost smoking hot before adding your batter. This is just as important as your batter recipe.

We have found that when keeping the traditional Yorkshire puddings hot through service that they can dry up, and we read somewhere that beer was used to keep them moist years ago. So we started looking into this and came up with a recipe that we have found is more like a pudding.

The best way to serve Yorkshire puddings, whichever recipe you are using, is straight from the oven, but for our purposes we have found that this recipe holds better during service and would be better if you do want to make your puddings in advance. We find that the taste is good too!

Ingredients:

300ml   beer (bitter)
100ml   Jersey milk
450ml   free range eggs
400g   plain flour
salt and pepper

Method:

1. Mix the flour and the eggs well, with a whisk. Add the salt and pepper and gradually whisk in the milk and beer. If necessary pass the mixture through a conical strainer (if you start with the eggs and flour this is usually not necessary).
2. Heat your trays in the oven to 200°C, with a little vegetable oil in each dish (you can use beef or duck dripping if you prefer). When almost smoking, ¾ fill the dishes with the Yorkshire pudding batter, and close the door immediately. They will take 25-30 minutes.
3. Don't open the door and they should rise to double the original size. Note that the puddings made by this recipe will not rise as much as those made by the milk recipe and will have a far more cakey texture.

To serve:

Serve with slim slices of roast rib beef, roast gravy and horseradish sauce. We also serve ours as canapés.

Chef's tip:

It is best to make this mixture 2-3 hours in advance and give it a good whisk just before using it. The mixture can also be made the day before it is needed and left in the fridge overnight.

spicy tempura of baby back ribs with ginger dipping sauce

This rib recipe is also really good on the barbecue as well as a tempura. The rib glaze mentioned below is usually stocked by butchers and we use a Peking glaze. We also buy a barbecue sauce base and have found that there are some excellent ready made sauces on the market.

Ingredients:

2	racks baby back ribs (12 bone racks)
	MIX TOGETHER:
100ml	Sweet chilli sauce (your favourite brand)
200ml	barbecue sauce (your favourite brand)
30g	powdered rib glaze (ask your butcher)
30g	honey
	salt and pepper

Method:

1. Season the racks with salt and pepper then rub the mix all over, both sides of the racks. Place them on a roasting tray and cover with tin foil. Place into a preheated oven at 140°C for 2 hours and 20 minutes.
2. Check that the meat comes away from the bone and allow to cool.
3. Slice the ribs into individual bone ribs, lightly dust them with seasoned flour then dip them into the tempura batter (see recipe on page 203).
4. Place them in the deep fryer at 175°C for 4 minutes, drain on a kitchen towel.

tempura seasoning

Ingredients:

2 tbsp	salt
1 tbsp	ground white pepper
2 tbsp	five spice

Method:

1. Mix all the ingredients together.

chilli ginger dipping sauce

Ingredients:

50ml	soy sauce
100ml	rice wine
100ml	rice vinegar
50g	sugar
1dstspn	ginger, grated
1 tbsp	red chillies (chopped)
2 tbsp	coriander (chopped)

Method:

1. Bring all the ingredients to the boil and simmer for 2 minutes.
2. Allow to cool and add the grated ginger, chopped red chillies and chopped coriander.

To serve:

Season with a little tempura seasoning and serve with the dipping sauce.

Suggested drink:

These are so incredibly moreish that we suggest you enjoy them with whatever is your favourite drink. Otherwise – drink tap water!

thai style coconut and peanut beef curry

Ingredients:

600g	diced chuck steak (lean)
1 tsp	ginger
60g	raw unsalted peanuts
1 tbsp	red chillies (finely chopped)
500ml	coconut milk
½ tsp	Thai red curry paste
4	medium shallots (peeled and sliced)
1	clove garlic (crushed)
20g	palm sugar (crushed)
1 tsp	fish sauce
1	medium lemon grass (sliced)
1	lime leaf (sliced)
2 tbsp	vegetable oil

zest and juice of 1 lime
handful of coriander leaves
pinch of salt

Method:

1. In a medium sized saucepan heat the vegetable oil and add the chuck steak. Fry for 2-3 minutes, add the curry paste, shallots, garlic and ginger and continue to cook for 1 more minute. Season with a little salt then add 40g of the peanuts, the lemon grass, lime leaf and palm sugar followed by the coconut milk. Bring to the boil.
2. Cover with a lid and place in a preheated oven at 160°C for 2 hours.
3. Remove from the oven and bring back to the boil on the stove top.
4. Finish with the lime zest and juice, fish sauce and a sprinkling of roughly chopped coriander.
5. Serve with boiled jasmine rice and the remainder of the peanuts lightly roasted.

Suggested drink:

Light lager beer, fruity white wine or a Rock Shandy (soda, lemonade and angostura bitters with lime and lots of ice).

Illustration using
Jersey Pottery Partiri and Helix range

139

slow pot roast leg of jersey lamb with rosemary and garlic, served with milky mashed potatoes

Serves 4-6

The slow roasting method helps to achieve a succulent melt in the mouth lamb dish that just flakes off the bone.

Ingredients:

1 x 2.5 kg	leg of lamb
100ml	white wine
100ml	water
50ml	olive oil
12 cloves	garlic (skin left on)
4-5 sprigs	rosemary
4-5 sprigs	thyme
salt and pepper	

Method:

1. Lay the leg of lamb skin side up in a casserole dish, season with salt and pepper. Sprinkle the garlic over the leg of lamb, then spoon over the water, white wine and olive oil.
2. Sprinkle the herbs on top, place a lid on the dish and place in a pre heated oven at 180°C for 1 ½ hours. Then reduce the heat to 140°C for a further 1 ¾ hours.

milky mash

Ingredients:

800g	waxy potatoes (cut into even sized pieces)
2 tbsp	salt, plus more to taste
100g	Jersey unsalted butter
125ml	Jersey milk
ground pepper	

Suggested wine:

You can't go wrong with a full bodied Rioja Reserva; smooth, soft, rich, heavenly!

Method:

1. Place the potatoes in a saucepan, fill up with water, about 2 inches above the potatoes, add the salt.
2. Bring to the boil and then simmer for about 20 minutes so the potatoes are just cooked. Drain them in a colander then put them through a potato ricer or mash them with a home style potato masher. Be careful not to beat it for too long as it will become gloopy.
3. Put the mash back onto the heat and gradually beat in the butter and the milk. This potato dish is quite wet, so season with more salt if required and add the ground pepper.

To serve:

Break up or slice the lamb and serve with some of the juices, garlic cloves and mash.

meatballs with tomato and basil

Ingredients:

400g	minced beef
100g	minced pork
50g	parmesan (shaved)
1	egg
2	cloves Garlic (chopped)
2 tbsp	Olive oil
1 tsp	Dijon mustard
1 tsp	Fresh mixed herbs – rosemary thyme and basil (chopped)
400ml	basic tomato sauce (see page 72)

zest of 1 lemon
salt and pepper

To serve:

grated parmesan
a few picked basil leaves

Method:

1. To make the meatballs lightly mix all the ingredients, without overworking them too much as it will make them rubbery when cooked. Place the mix into the refrigerator for at least 1 hour then mould the mix into 24 little meatballs.
2. Allow to firm up in the fridge for at least 2 hours. This mix also freezes well.
3. In a large casserole pot add 2 tablespoons of olive oil and heat over a moderate heat. Add the meatballs and fry for 2 minutes or so, just to start the cooking process, turning the meatballs over as you fry.
4. Remove some of the excess fat then add the tomato sauce. Bring to the boil, cover with a lid and place in a preheated oven (190°C) for 20 minutes.

To serve:

Serve with cooked linguine, grated parmesan and fresh basil leaves.

Suggested wine:

Full bodied Italian. Go for a great value Valpolicella; soft and packed with fruit.

142

basic pasta

Ingredients:

500g   flour (preferably '00' flour)
6   medium egg yolks
4   whole medium eggs
pinch of salt

Method:

1. Sieve the flour into a large bowl, add the salt and make a well in the middle.
2. Whisk all the eggs together and pour into the well of the flour.
3. Gradually bring the flour into the eggs by using one hand. Bind it together and knead into a dough.
4. Cut the dough in half.
5. Securely cling film both halves of the dough and put it in the fridge for about an hour. (It will last in the fridge for a day before oxidizing, when it will become un-usable.)
6. The pasta is then ready to roll.

masterclass:
crab ravioli

Method:

1. Spoon/divide the crab mix onto the rolled pasta sheets.
2. Brush a little water around the filling, this will help the two layers stick together.
3. Place the next layer of pasta on top, ensuring the two layers stick together, squeezing the air out as you go.
4. Use a small cutter upside down to seal the sides of the pasta together.
5. With a large cutter, cut the ravioli out.
6. Lay the ravioli on a floured baking tray ready to cook.

145

masterclass: tortellini

1. Cut the pasta with a large cutter.
2. Spoon a little mix on the pasta circles.
3. Brush a little water around the mix and then fold them over to form a crescent.
4. Roll around your finger to create tortellini.
5. Layer the tortellini on a floured tray.
6. Cook in boiling, salted water.
7. Drain and mix with shallots and crispy bacon or pancetta.

pigeon and porcini tortellini

Serves 4, makes between 8 to 12

Ingredients:

1   pigeon
30g   dried porcini mushrooms
          (soaked in water for
          10 minutes and
          chopped)
150ml   veal/beef stock reduced
          to one third volume (see
          recipe on page 201)
2 tbsp   onion
1 tsp   garlic (chopped)
½ tsp   thyme (chopped)
50ml   Madeira (see recipe on
          page 201)
1   rasher thick bacon/
          pancetta (cut into strips)
30g   unsalted Jersey butter
½   quantity of basic pasta
          (see masterclass on
          page 144)
salt and pepper

Suggested wine:

We would love to drink
Guidalberto, Tenuto San Guido,
second wine of the acclaimed
Sassicaia vineyard.

Method:

1. Season the pigeon with salt and pepper. Heat a small pan and seal the pigeon all over and place into a preheated oven at 190°C for 8 to 10 minutes. This will cook it medium rare. Remove from oven and allow to cool slightly.
2. In a saucepan melt the butter and add the onion, garlic and thyme and cook over a medium heat.
3. Add the bacon and cook for a minute of so.
4. Increase the heat and add the Madeira and reduce until it has all evaporated.
5. Add the porcini mushrooms and beef stock and a little of the liquid from the mushrooms and reduce by half.
6. Once the pigeon is cool enough to handle, remove from the bone and dice into small pieces.
7. When the sauce is cold, mix two thirds with the pigeon.
8. Keep the mixture in the fridge until ready to use.
9. To make the tortellini you need a pasta machine. Cut the pasta into 4 pieces then lightly dust with flour. Roll out with a rolling pin until it is at a thickness that will go through the pasta machine. Dusting with flour regularly, keep putting the pasta through the machine, slowly going through the numbers and reducing the thickness.
10. Dust with flour all the time, until you get to the thinnest setting, lay the pasta on a floured table. Along the sheet of pasta put a small piece of the stuffing in the centre cutting the pasta with a cutter.
11. Then fold each parcel in half, roll it around your finger and twist, as illustrated in the pictures on page 146.
12. To cook, place the tortellini in a sauce pan of boiling salted water for 2-3 minutes until firm to the bite.
13. Remove from the water and brush with olive oil.

To serve:

Serve with some shallots, crispy bacon or pancetta and Madeira sauce.

crab and ginger ravioli

Serves 4 to 6

Ingredients:

200g	picked crab
½ tsp	fresh grated ginger
2 tbsp	double cream
1 tbsp	mascarpone cheese
1 tbsp	grated parmesan
4 tbsp	chopped parsley
1 tbsp	olive oil
½	quantity of basic pasta, (see masterclass on page 144)
1	tomato (chopped)

salt and pepper to season
a few basil leaves to garnish

Method:

1. Mix all the ingredients together and place in the fridge to firm up for at least 1 hour.
2. To make the ravioli you need a pasta machine, any good cook shop will sell them. Cut the pasta into 4 pieces then lightly dust with flour. Roll out with a rolling pin until it is at a thickness that will go through the pasta machine. Dusting with flour regularly, keep putting the pasta through the machine, slowly going through the numbers and reducing the thickness.
3. Dust with flour all the time, until you get to the thinnest setting, lay the pasta on a floured table. Along the sheet of pasta put a small piece of the stuffing in the centre leaving 5cm or so either side of the stuffing, brush around the stuffing with a little water then roll out another sheet of pasta and lay it over the top pressing around each ravioli.
4. Cut the ravioli out, leaving approximately 2cm of pasta overlapping.
5. To cook, bring a saucepan of water to a rolling boil, add a good pinch of salt then drop the raviolis in. Reduce to a simmer, and cook for about 2 minutes.

To serve:

Drain and serve with a little lemon butter (see recipe on page 200) with a little chopped tomato and some basil leaves.

Suggested wine:

Savennieres from the Loire.

Illustration using
Bespoke ceramics for Oyster Box Jersey

cheese

We use cheese from across the globe as the diversity in our business allows us to stock all sorts of cheese. The selection ranges from Buffalo Mozzarella used in Anti Pasti buffets and simple salads for our cafés, to good quality British cheeses such as Montgomery and Lincolnshire Poachers. We use Parmesan or Gran Padano for a wide range of dishes and a good variety of goats' cheese.

When compiling a cheese menu or cheese board you need a good balance. A good cheese board would incorporate five varieties, one blue, one soft, one hard, one goats' and one different to all the others. We also like to have a variety of cheeses from different countries.

As with wine, we believe that with cheese you generally get what you pay for and we can't say strongly enough that many of the processed cheeses that are purchased from large supermarkets are not that good for eating, although they may have their uses in cooking! Good cheese may seem expensive – but a little does go a long way!

A small plate of excellent farmhouse cheese, served with good bread, and chutney, makes a fabulous light meal or snack.

jersey cheese

There are some superb cheeses made from Jersey milk and in fact there is a World Jersey Cheese Festival held annually. It is a much-anticipated event on the Jersey calendar, held in conjunction with the Foire de Jersey.

The three-day festival takes place at the Royal Jersey Showground in the parish of Trinity, the rural heart of the island, with the focal point of the festival being the World Jersey Cheese Awards.

It is a major competitive event for the dairy trade. It is believed that this is the first competition of its kind, consisting solely of cheese made from the milk of a single breed of cow, the Jersey Cow. Each year cheeses are shipped from all corners of the globe to Jersey to be judged. For more information visit www.royaljersey.co.uk

camembert

1. An interesting way to enjoy camembert is to cut it straight through the middle from the side. For a 250g camembert, spread 1 tablespoon of apple chutney (see recipe on page 203) over the centre of the camembert, then sprinkle over some mint and basil leaves.
2. Slice one fig finely and spread that over the camembert then place the two halves together, like a sandwich.
3. Place in the fridge with a weight on top for at least an hour or so.
4. Remove from the fridge at least an hour before serving.
5. The camembert goes fantastically well with our oatmeal biscuits (see recipe on page154).

Illustration using
Jersey Pottery WineSpeak and Cheese range

153

oatmeal biscuits
for cheese

Ingredients:

200g   wholemeal flour
200g   porridge oats
50g   sugar
25g   butter (slightly softened)
2   free range eggs
20g   cumin seeds
pinch of salt
pinch of bicarbonate of soda

Method:

1. Mix all the dry ingredients together then, with your hands, flake in the butter.
2. Add the beaten eggs and blend. Divide the mix into 20 balls and rest them in the fridge for ½ an hour.
3. Lightly dust with flour. Roll the biscuits out and lay them on a greased baking tray.
4. Preheat the oven to 185°C and bake the biscuits for 12 minutes.

155

poached pear with chocolate pavlova

Serves 4

for the pear

Ingredients:

4	pears
1	lime
4	passion fruits
5g	fresh ginger
30ml	grenadine syrup
400ml	water
150g	sugar

Method:

1. Cut the lime in two and squeeze the juice into a pan, adding the fruit.
2. Scoop out the fruit flesh of the passion fruit into the pan too and add the peeled, sliced ginger, grenadine syrup, water and sugar.
3. Bring the syrup to the boil.
4. Peel and core the pears leaving them whole.
5. Add them to the boiling syrup, cover the pan and slowly poach until they are tender.
6. Remove the pears form the syrup until everything has cooled down, to avoid overcooking.

for the pavlova

Ingredients:

200g	egg whites
200g	sugar
100g	light brown sugar
100g	icing sugar
25g	cornflour
30g	cocoa powder

Method:

1. Preheat the oven to 130°C, leaving the baking tray in the oven to heat through.
2. Mix egg whites and caster sugar in a mixing bowl and place over a pot with simmering water.
3. Heat the mix while continuously stirring until it reaches approximately 70°C.
4. Make sure the eggs don't catch on the bowl .
5. Remove from the heat and whisk the egg whites until stiff.
6. Add the light brown sugar and mix in well.
7. Sieve the icing sugar, cocoa powder and the cornflour together and fold into the egg whites.
8. Pipe four large adjoining dots onto baking paper.
9. Carefully pull the pavlovas onto the hot baking tray and put in the oven.
10. Turn down the temperature to 100°C and cook for 35 minutes.

for the walnut cream

Ingredients:

150g	sugar
3 tbsp	water
60g	walnut pieces
250g	double cream
30g	sugar

Suggested wine:

Orange Muscat and Flora, Brown Brothers.

Method:

1. Add the water to the sugar in a pan and bring to the boil.
2. Cook until the sugar becomes caramel.
3. Add the walnuts and mix well with the caramel.
4. To avoid the caramel becoming too firm, keep stirring while on the heat.
5. Spead the caramel onto baking paper and leave to cool.
6. When cold, crush the praline with a rolling pin or in a food processor.
7. Whip the cream with the sugar to a soft peak and add the walnut praline.

To serve the pears:

1. Reduce the syrup from the pears to make a sauce.
2. Pipe a spiral of walnut cream onto the plate and lean the meringue on one side.
3. Slice the pears on the bottom and add to the side of the cream.
4. Decorate with some of the syrup and dust with icing sugar.

pink grapefruit and cinnamon posset

Serves 4

for the posset

Ingredients:

600g	double cream
150g	caster sugar
2	pink grapefruits
½	lemon
1	stick cinnamon

Method:

1. Place sugar, cinnamon and cream into a pan and gently heat up to just below simmering.
2. Leave to steep and cool down. With a peeler cut off strips of grapefruit zest and put to the side.
3. Sqeeze the grapefruit and lemon juice through a sieve to make 200ml.
4. Remove the cinnamon from the cream and add the grapefruit juice.
5. Mix well and fill into serving glasses making 4 portions.
6. Leave in fridge overnight.

for the syrup

Ingredients:

4 tbsp sugar
6 tbsp water
grapefruit zest

Method:

1. Bring the sugar and water to the boil, add the grapefruit zest and keep boiling until it becomes a thick syrup.
2. Cover and leave to marinate overnight.

for the decoration

Ingredients:

2	pink grapefruits
4	eggs
200g	icing sugar
200g	plain flour
lemon essence	
vanilla essence	

Method:

1. Peel the 2 remaining grapefruits.
2. Remove the grapefruit peel from the syrup and roll it in some caster sugar.
3. Sift the flour and icing sugar together and add some vanilla and lemon flavour to it.
4. Add the eggs and mix well.
5. Prepare a stencil cut from 1mm thick plastic or carton.
6. Grease a non stick tray and place stencil on it.
7. Spread a little tuille mix (see recipe on page 160) with a pallet knife over the stencil and pull the plastic off.
8. Make several biscuits and cook them in a hot oven (190°C).
9. Watch them cook and take from oven when the sides start to brown.
10. While still hot, twist them around a pencil or a wooden cooking spoon to form a spiral.

Suggested wine:

Champagne Laurent-Perrier, Demi sec.

To serve:

Place two grapefruit segments on top of the posset and decorate with the sugared zest and the tuille. Recipes for chocolate decorations can be found on page 178.

Illustration using
Jersey Pottery Kate's Cakes range

159

rum and raisin crème brûlée

Serves 4

Ingredients:

80g	raisins (best quality available)
80g	dark rum (best quality available)
100g	golden caster sugar
150g	egg yolks
½	vanilla pod
500g	whipping cream
golden caster sugar, to dust	

Method:

1. Marinate the raisins in the rum for at least one day.
2. Slit open the vanilla pod, scrape out the seeds and add to the cream.
3. Bring the cream to boiling point.
4. Drain the raisins, keeping the rum.
5. Whisk egg yolks, sugar and the rum from the raisins together and slowly add the hot cream to it while stirring.
6. Pour the mix through a fine sieve and into the desired dishes, like ramekins or glasses.
7. Sprinkle over the raisins and cook the brûlées in a preheated oven at 100°C until just set. This can be checked by slightly rocking the dish to see if the centre has set.
8. Place in fridge to chill.

Ingredients for the tuille:

4	eggs
200g	icing sugar
200g	plain flour
lemon essence	
vanilla essence	

Method:

1. Sift the flour and icing sugar together and add some vanilla and lemon flavour to it.
2. Add the eggs and mix well.
3. Prepare a stencil cut from 1mm thick plastic or carton.
4. Grease a non stick tray and place stencil on it.
5. Spread a little tuille mix with a pallet knife over the stencil and pull the plastic off.
6. Make several biscuits and cook them in a hot oven (190°C).
7. Watch them cook and take from oven when the sides start to brown.
8. When oven hot, wrap around the handle of a wooden spoon or pencil to make a cigar. If you would like to dip the tuille in chocolate, see page 178 for the method for tempering chocolate.

Suggested drink:

Muscat de Rivesaltes, Domaine Cazes.

To serve:

Sprinkle some golden caster sugar on top of each crème brûlée and caramelise the sugar using a blow torch. Serve with some more raisins and the tuille biscuits.

Illustration using
Jersey Pottery Partiri and Helix range

passion fruit and ginger panna cotta

Serves 8

Ingredients:

18	fresh passion fruits
140g	caster sugar
60g	fresh ginger root (peeled and cut into chunky pieces)
800g ̀	whipping cream
5	gelatine leaves
200g	soured cream/crème fraîche
8	portion moulds

Method:

1. Remove the pulp from the passion fruits and place into a pan. Add the caster sugar and the ginger root.
2. Bring this fruit mix to the boil and simmer a little until it shows syrup consistency.
3. Add the cream to it and return to the heat to bring the cream to a light simmer.
4. Meanwhile, soak the gelatine leaves in cold water until soft, squeeze excess water out and add to the hot cream. Mix well until gelatine is dissolved and add the crème fraîche. Again mix well to make a smooth mix and strain it through a sieve to remove the pips and the ginger. Fill straight into the moulds and place in fridge until set.

To serve:

Remove the panna cotta from its mould, by placing the mould into hot water, only for a couple of seconds until the sides get loose, then turning over. Knock until the panna cotta slips out and place it onto a plate. Decorate with sauce, tuille biscuits (see recipe on page 160) and your choice of fruit.

Suggested drink:

Jersey Pottery blend coffee,
roasted by Cooper & Co of Jersey.

Illustration using
Jersey Pottery Strip range

163

lime and vodka parfait

Serves 6

Ingredients:

2	limes
70g	brown sugar
4	shot vodka
90g	egg whites
170g	light brown sugar
40g	water
500g	whipping cream

Method:

1. Cut the limes into halves and add the vodka and the 70g brown sugar.
2. In a food processor smash up the limes so that the juices come out and strain through a sieve, collecting the juices.
3. Bring 130g of the light brown sugar and the water to the boil and cook until it reaches 115°C.
4. Meanwhile, place the egg whites into a mixerbowl and add the remaining 40g of light brown sugar. Whisk until light.
5. When the sugar and water has reached temperature, slowly add it to the egg whites while beating.
6. Continue whisking until the meringue is cold.
7. Now fold the juices and the whipped cream into the meringue and fill into desired moulds.
8. Place in freezer over night.

To serve:

Make skewers from exotic fruits like pineapple, kiwi, mango, paw paw etc. and drizzle some fresh passion fruit over them. Remove the parfait from its mould and place onto a plate. Place the fruit skewer onto the plate and serve with shortbread (see recipe on page 198) or tuille biscuits (see recipe on page 160).

Suggested drink:

Iced blackcurrant vodka.

roasted apple parfait

Serves 6

for the praline wafer

Ingredients:

300g	sugar
4 tbsp	water
120g	flaked almonds

Method:

1. Add the water to the sugar in a pan and bring to the boil.
2. Cook until the sugar becomes caramel.
3. Add the almonds and mix well with the caramel.
4. To avoid the caramel becoming too firm, keep stirring while on the heat.
5. When the caramel is smooth, spread 8 wafers onto silicon or baking paper using either a silicon spatula or a greased spoon. Make sure to make very thin wafers.
6. Spead the remaining caramel onto the paper and leave to cool.
7. When cold, crush the remaining praline with a rolling pin or in a food processor .
8. If you would like to make the wafers rounded, cut the paper into 4 pieces to accommodate the wafers and place in a hot oven (150°C) to make the caramel soft again. Remove from the oven and place over a bottle or a rolling pin to form the desired shape.

for the parfait

Ingredients:

300g	apples (peeled and cored)
75g	sugar
¼ tsp	cinnamon
60g	Australian sultanas
30g	Calvados
30g	condensed milk
90g	egg yolks
60g	sugar
60g	praline (leftover from wafer)
600ml	whipped double cream

Method:

1. Soak the sultanas in Calvados 2 days ahead.
2. Slice apples into wedges and mix with the sugar and cinnamon then cook in the oven until soft.
3. Drain off the juice from the cooked apples, keeping 60g, and leave to cool down.
4. Mix the juice with the condensed milk and bring to the boil.
5. Whisk egg yolks and sugar together until light and add the boiling milk.
6. Now whisk until cold.
7. Fold apples, the marinated sultanas, praline and whipped cream carefully into the egg mixture.
8. Pour the mixture into a square tin lined with paper and cling film straight away.
9. With a scraper, make a design on the top of the parfait (see picture).

for the sauce

Ingredients:

3	oranges
150g	sugar

Method:

1. Peel off large strips of orange zest and remove all white from the inside of the zest.
2. Cut into very thin strips along the long side of the zest.
3. Squeeze the juice, placing in a pan along with the peel strips and the sugar and bring to the boil.
4. Reduce the syrup slowly until ca. half remains.

Suggested wine:
Sauternes.

To serve:

Cut the parfait into cubes and place onto the plate. Decorate the plate with the sauce, a sprinkle of cinnamon and the praline wafer and serve straight away.

cheeky raspberry meringue tart

Serves 8 to 10

for the base

Ingredients:
200g   crushed digestive biscuits
110g   melted butter

Method:
1. Place a flan ring of 24cm diameter onto a piece of greaseproof paper and wrap the excess around the sides of the ring.
2. Place onto a cake card.
3. Mix the melted butter into the digestive biscuits and dress the flan ring and base with the mix.

for the cream filling

Ingredients:
110g   raspberries fresh or frozen
30g   caster sugar
110g   yoghurt
5g   gelatine
200g   whipped double cream

Method:
1. Soak the gelatine in cold water.
2. Place the raspberries and the sugar in a pan and, while stirring, warm up until the sugar is dissolved, then place into a mixing bowl.
3. Squeeze excess water from the gelatine and place into the pan used for the raspberries, melt slowly on the heat until hot, but not boiling!
4. Mix the yoghurt into the raspberries, then stir in the hot gelatine mixing well and quickly, then fold in the whipped cream.
5. Fill the mousse into the prepared biscuit base and spread out using a pallet knife.
6. Decorate the centre of the tart with fresh raspberries.
7. Place in fridge to set for at least 2 hours.

for the meringue

Ingredients:
150g   egg whites
150g   caster sugar
75g   light brown sugar
75g   icing sugar
20g   cornflour

Method:
1. Mix egg whites and caster sugar in a mixing bowl and place over a pot with simmering water.
2. Heat the mix while continuously stirring until it reaches approximately 70°C.
3. Remove from the heat and whisk the egg whites until stiff.
4. Add the light brown sugar and mix in well.
5. Sieve the icing sugar and the cornflour together and fold into the egg whites.
6. Fill meringue into a piping bag with a round nozzle and pipe around the sides.
7. With a blow torch, caramelise the meringue evenly from all sides .
8. To finish the raspberry tart, mix the water and raspberry jam and bring it the boil in a pan. Strain through a sieve and glaze the raspberries with it.

to finish

Ingredients:

2 tbsp water
4 tbsp raspberry jam

Suggested wine:
Sauternes.

Illustration using
Jersey Pottery Kate's Cakes range

cheeky little tarts

mille-feuilles of poached apples and brandy snap biscuits

Serves 6

for the apples

Ingredients:

6	medium size tart apples like braeburn
120g	caster sugar
pinch	cinnamon
pinch	nutmeg
	A little water
	vanilla pod
8 tbsp	Jersey apple brandy from La Mare

Method:
1. Peel, core and cut the apples into halves, then into 1cm thick slices.
2. Place in a pan and add the sugar, cinnamon and nutmeg.
3. Slit open the vanilla pod and remove the seeds into a mixer bowl.
4. Add the empty vanilla pod to the apples and add some water to start the cooking process.
5. Cover the pan with a lid and gently cook the apples on a low heat until just soft.
6. Add the apple brandy, heat through a little and then set it on fire with a lighter or blow torch to flambé the apples.
7. Pour out into a bowl or tray to leave to cool.

for the brandy snap biscuits

Ingredients:

25g	plain flour
25g	golden syrup
1 tsp	ground ginger
50g	caster sugar
50g	butter
1 tbsp	apple brandy
200g	white chocolate
30ml	walnut oil

Method:
1. Melt the butter, sugar and golden syrup together.
2. Mix the flour and ginger and add to the butter mix along with the apple brandy. Leave the mix to set until it can be shaped into 18 balls.
3. Place the balls onto a non stick tray and cook at 180°C for 5-7 minutes until golden and crisp.
4. While still hot, cut into circles of 7cm diameter, using a plain cutter.
5. Gently melt the white chocolate and walnut oil together, making sure the chocolate does not get too warm.
6. When the biscuits are cold, dip them into the white chocolate and let any excess chocolate run off before placing them on the baking parchment.
7. For the chocolate to set quicker, put the biscuits in the fridge.

for the cream

Ingredients:

500ml	double cream
50ml	la mare, jersey apple brandy
4 tbsp	La Mare, Jersey black butter
2 tbsp	caster sugar

Method:

Whisk the cream and vanilla seeds to soft peaks and add the black butter, sugar, apple brandy, folding and mixing everything gently together.

To serve:

Place one biscuit on each plate and layer with a conelle of the black butter cream and 3 slices of apples, topping with a biscuit. Repeat the layering and finish with a biscuit and a small conelle of cream for decoration. If you wish, you can decorate with any broken pieces of brandy snap.
Arrange 3 slices of apples on the side of the mille-feuilles and drizzle cooking juices from the apples around the sides.

Suggested wine:

Muscat des Baumes des Venise.

jersey black butter cheesecake

Serves 8

Ingredients:

300g	digestive biscuits
100g	unsalted butter
1 jar/225g	La Mare Jersey black butter (or any high fruit content jam)
1	vanilla pod (split and seeds scraped)
3 tbsp	water
juice of ½ lemon	
4	gelatine leaves
500ml	double cream
300g	Philadelphia cream cheese

Method:

1. Blend the digestive biscuits and butter in a food processor until fine crumbs are formed.
2. Press into an 8 inch flan ring to make the base for the cheesecake.
3. Soak the gelatine in cold water.
4. Whisk the double cream to a soft peak and place it into the fridge.
5. Split the vanilla pod lengthways and scrape the seeds out into a bowl, adding the cream cheese and black butter. Gently whisk the ingredients together to make a smooth base for the cheesecake.
6. Heat the water and the lemon juice in a pan until it simmers.
7. Drain and squeeze the gelatine, remove the pan from the heat and whisk in the gelatine.
8. Add to the black butter and Philadelphia mix and fold in.
9. Remove the double cream from the fridge and fold it into the Philadelphia mix.
10. Add the cheesecake mix to the lined ring, spread and smooth out with a pallet knife and refrigerate for at least 2 hours.
11. Run a hot knife around the sides of the cake ring to remove the cheesecake and decorate with anything you fancy.

Suggested wine:

Freshly brewed, black Earl Grey tea.

Illustration using
Jersey Pottery Kate's Cakes range

saucy helene pear tart

Serves 8 to 10

for the base

Ingredients:

90g	melted butter
30g	melted dark chocolate
180g	crushed digestive biscuits

Method:
1. Place a flan ring of 20cm diameter onto a piece of greaseproof paper and wrap the excess around the sides of the ring.
2. Place onto a cake card.
3. Mix the melted butter and chocolate into the digestive biscuits and dress the flan ring and base with the mix.

for the filling

Ingredients:

4	pears (peeled, cored and cut into halves)
250g	caster sugar
400ml	water
½	vanilla pod
¼	lemon, juice only
20g	caster sugar
20g	pear syrup
30g	egg yolks (2)
300g	whipped cream
½	vanilla pod
2	leaves gelatine

Method:
1. Slit open the vanilla pod and, with the back of your knife, scrape out the seeds.
2. Bring the water with the vanilla seed and pod, caster sugar and lemon juice to the boil.
3. Add the pears to the syrup, cover and simmer until the pears are soft.
4. Remove the pears form the syrup and leave to cool.
5. Meanwhile soak the gelatine in cold water.
6. Mix the caster sugar, pear syrup, egg yolks and vanilla seeds from the second half in a mixer bowl and place over a pan with simmering water.
7. Bring to about 70ºC while continuously whisking, then remove from the heat.
8. Squeeze excess water from the gelatine and dissolve in the hot egg mixture.
9. Keep whisking frequently until the mix has cooled to room temperature and fold in the whipped cream in 2 batches.
10. Fill into the biscuit base and spread to give a rustic look.
11. Stick the pears decoratively into the cream and place in fridge to chill until set.

for the chocolate sauce and decoration

Ingredients:

100g	large, curly chocolate shards
100g	whipping cream
80g	dark chocolate in small pieces
30ml	water
15g	cocoa powder
15g	sugar

Method:
1. Bring the water and the cream to boiling point.
2. Stir in the sieved cocoa powder and cook gently for one minute.
3. Add the chocolate and mix until the sauce is smooth.
4. To finish the tart sprinkle the milk chocolate shards around the side of the tart. Serve with the hot chocolate sauce.

Suggested wine:

Klein Constantia, Vin de Constance.

Illustration using
Jersey Pottery Kate's Cakes range

175

orange charlotte

Serves 6

Ingredients:

for the sides

6	oranges (like blood oranges)
500ml	water
250g	sugar
1 pack	sponge finger biscuits

for the cream

250ml	freshly squeezed orange juice
100g	egg yolks
100g	sugar
1	vanilla pod
5	leaves gelatine
600g	whipped cream

Method:

1. Wash the oranges and thinly slice off about 30 slices for decoration.
2. Bring the water and the sugar to the boil and add the orange slices.
3. Cook the oranges on a gentle heat until the syrup has reduced to a stock syrup consistency.
4. Remove from the heat and leave to cool and marinate overnight.
5. Soak the gelatine in cold water.
6. Slit open the vanilla pod and scrape the seeds into the pan along with the pod.
7. Bring the orange juice and vanilla to the boil.
8. Simmer and reduce to make 230g of syrup.
9. Mix egg yolks with some orange juice in a round bowl and add the hot syrup, mixing well.
10. Place the bowl over a pot with simmering water and, while stirring continuously bring to 70°C again.
11. Remove from the heat and add the soaked and squeezed gelatine, stir well and leave to cool until it has set.
12. In the meantime line 6 individual mousse rings with strips of baking parchment to cover the sides.
13. Place 4 slices of the syrup oranges round the side of the rings.
14. Cut the sponge finger biscuits to size and fit into the base of the charlottes.
15. Now add the whipped cream to the egg mix in two batches and fill into a piping bag with a large star nozzle.
16. Fill up the mousse rings with the cream and pipe a separate peak of cream on top.

To serve:

Remove the ring and paper and place the charlotte on a plate. Decorate the plate with the syrup from the oranges and some double cream. If you would like to serve it with a tuille, see page 160 for a recipe.

Suggested wine:

Klein Constantia, Vin de Constance.
This wine is so good we recommend it twice!

Season: Summer / Early Autumn

white chocolate bavarois
with fresh berries

Serves 8

for the sponge base

Ingredients

200g	eggs
100g	sugar
65g	flour
35g	cornflour

Method:

1. Whisk eggs and sugar until fluffy and white.
2. Sift the flour and cornflour together and carefully fold into egg mix.
3. Spread out onto a sheet of baking paper to fit your tray.
4. Cook at 180°C for approximately 7 minutes.

for the bavarois

Ingredients:

60g	egg yolks
250g	milk
50g	sugar
200g	white chocolate (best quality, in small pieces)
6	gelatine leaves
1	vanilla pod
600ml	whipping cream, whipped

Method:

1. Soak the gelatine in cold water.
2. Cut a disc of 7 inches in diameter from the sponge roulade and fit it into a same size mousse ring.
3. Combine egg yolks, sugar and milk in a round bowl.
4. Slit open the vanilla pod to remove the seeds and add both the pod and the seeds to the milk.
5. Place over a pan with simmering water and bring the mix to 70°C while continuously whisking.
6. Remove from the heat and add to the white chocolate.
7. Stir and leave to melt the chocolate for a minute, stir again to blend all ingredients well.
8. Squeeze excess water from the gelatine and add to the bavarois base, mix very well.
9. When the base has cooled down to room temperature, add the whipped cream bit by bit, folding it into the base.
10. Remove the vanilla pod.
11. Fill the mixture into the mousse ring and refrigerate for at least 4 hours.

for the decoration

Ingredients:

200g	white chocolate
200g	mixed fresh berries of your choice

Suggested wine:
Laurent-Perrier Rosé.

Method:

1. Melt 100g of the chocolate in a thin metal bowl over simmering water.
2. Cut the remaining 100g of chocolate into small pieces and add to the melted chocolate after removing the bowl from the heat.
3. Slowly stir until all chocolate is melted and the temperature of the chocolate has reached about 28°C, well under body temperature.
4. Spread the chocolate (not too thinly) onto baking paper, forming flower petal shapes – make enough to decorate the full circumference of the bavarois.
5. Spread the remaining chocolate onto a small piece of baking paper using a cranked pallet knife and when it starts to set, cut a butterfly shape from it.
6. To serve, run a hot knife around the side of the mousse ring, loosening the bavarois. Place onto a plate and decorate with the fresh berries and the butterfly.

Illustration using
Jersey Pottery Strawberries and Cream range

valrhona chocolate truffles

for chocolate disc

Ingredients:

300g   dark chocolate,
        Valrhona couverture

Method:

1. Melt 200g of the chocolate in a thin metal bowl over simmering water.
2. Cut the remaining 100g of chocolate into small pieces and add to the melted chocolate after removing the bowl from the heat.
3. Slowly stir until all chocolate is melted and the temperature of the chocolate has reached about 30°C, just under body temperature.
4. Spread the chocolate thinly onto baking paper, using a cranked pallet knife.
5. When the chocolate starts to set, cut small circles with a plain cutter .
6. Remove the circles from the paper when chocolate has fully set and place them on a tray, leaving enough space between each of them.

for the filling

Ingredients:

60g   egg yolks
60g   caster sugar
50g   water
300g   chocolate melted
250ml ½ double cream,
        ½ whipping cream
cocoa powder, to dust

Method:

1. Place the egg yolks in a mixer bowl.
2. Combine the caster sugar and the water in a pan and bring to the boil.
3. While whisking, add the boiling hot sugar syrup to the egg yolks, then whisk until cold and light, ideally using a machine.
4. Whip the cream.
5. Add the melted chocolate to the egg mixture and mix well, make sure the chocolate is not too cold, otherwise the cream will set in an instant.
6. Fold the cream into the mix.
7. Pipe a dome shape using a plain nozzle in a piping bag onto the chocolate discs.
8. Refrigerate the truffles for 30 minutes.
9. Remelt the remaining chocolate and repeat the process of tempering the chocolate, adding some cut pieces to the melted chocolate as above.
10. Dip the truffles into the chocolate and slip onto a sheet. of grease proof paper.
11. Dust slightly with cocoa powder or decorate with a shard of chocolate.
12. Serve with caramelised nuts and raspberries if you like.

Suggested drink:
Jersey Pottery special blend double espresso.

Illustration using
Jersey Pottery Steamy Delights range

doughnuts with gooey chocolate sauce and jersey vanilla ice cream

Ingredients:

400g   flour
6g   salt
20g   yeast
45g   sugar
45g   butter (softened and diced)
1   egg
200ml   warm water

Method:

1. Place the yeast in a bowl with a pinch of the sugar and the warm water. Add 2 tablespoons of the flour and leave in a warm place until the mixture becomes frothy.
2. Put the remainder of the ingredients in a large bowl and pour on the yeast mixture. Mix to a dough.
3. Lightly flour the work surface and knead the dough for about 4-5 minutes until it is smooth. Place it in a bowl, cover with a damp cloth and leave in a warm place to rise, it takes about 1 hour.
4. When well rested, remove from the bowl and on a floured surface, knock the air out of it. Mould to 30g pieces. Leave on a greased baking tray for 30 minutes.
5. Heat clean vegetable oil in the deep fat fryer to 170°C. Place the doughnuts in the oil. They will take approximately 4 minutes to cook and knead to be turned over halfway through cooking. Remove from the fryer and drain on a kitchen towel.

sugar coating

Ingredients:

75g   caster sugar
1 tsp   ground cinnamon
½ tsp   allspice
zest ½ orange

Method:

1. Mix all of the ingredients together

To serve:

Roll through the spiced sugar mix and the doughnuts are ready to serve with Jersey vanilla ice cream and a chocolate sauce (you could use the 'filling' recipe on page 180).

Suggested drink:
Jersey Pottery special blend cappucino.

Illustration using
Jersey Pottery Kate's Cakes range

183

retro walnut tart with baileys cream

Serves 8 to 10

Ingredients for the pastry:

400g	plain flour
8g	baking powder
200g	butter
120g	icing sugar
1	egg
3	egg yolks

Method:

1. Sift the flour and the baking powder onto the table.
2. Place the icing sugar, butter, egg and yolks in the middle, mix a little and bring all ingredients together to make a pastry.
3. wrap in film and chill in the fridge for 30 minutes.

Ingredients for the filling:

250g	caster sugar
4 tbsp	water
200g	cream
220g	marzipan
240g	roughly chopped walnuts
120g	sugar
	vanilla essence

Method:

1. Moisten the sugar with the water and cook until it turns to caramel.
2. Slowly add the cream bit by bit while stirring to make a smooth toffee.
3. Add the second caster sugar and fold in.
4. Now flake in the marzipan and mix well to dissolve the marzipan into the toffee, add the vanilla essence and the walnuts to the mix.
5. Leave to cool.
6. Roll out 2/3 of the pastry to approximately 5mm thick and line a cake mould with a loose base with the pastry, cutting off excess pastry around the rim of the tin.
7. Fill in the toffee mix and smooth out to the sides.
8. Roll out the remaining pastry to form a top for the tart.
9. Place the lid on top of the filling, sealing the pastry on the sides.
10. Brush the lid thinly with beaten egg and fold the pastry sides onto the pastry lid, press down lightly to make the pastry stick together.
11. Prick with a fork and brush again with egg wash.
12. Cook the tart in a preheated oven at 170°C for approximately 30 minutes until golden and before the filling overcooks.

Ingredients for the mascarpone:

200g	mascarpone
100g	double cream
100g	baileys
1 tbsp	golden caster sugar

Method:

1. Place all ingredients into a mixer bowl and slowly whisk until all is combined.
2. Beat a little until the cream starts to thicken.
3. Ideally leave the tart to set at room temperature overnight. Slice with a sharp knife and serve with a dollop of mascarpone cream.

Suggested wine:

Jersey Pottery special blend
coffee with Jersey Cream.

Illustration using
Jersey Pottery Strip range

dragon fly apple flan

Serves 8 to 10

Ingredients:

5	large apples (sour and firm)
60ml	dry cider
50g	demerara sugar
1	cinnmon sticks
½	vanilla pods
340g	butter, soft
225g	light brown sugar
110g	caster sugar
6	eggs
1	pinch salt
340g	white flour
½ tsp	baking powder
1 tsp	ground cinnamon
1 tsp	ground cardamoms
½ tsp	ground ginger

Method:

1. Peel and core 4 apples and slice into thin wedges.
2. Add cider, demerara sugar and spices to the apples and steam on the stove until soft.
3. Drain off, keep the juices and leave the apples to cool.
4. Reduce the juices to a thin syrup consistency and leave on the side.
5. Cream the butter, salt and sugars together and add the eggs.
6. Sift the flour with the spices and fold all ingredients into the butter mix.
7. Place into a 10 inch Aga flan dish and spread out.
8. Peel, core and slice the remaining apple and use to decorate the top of the flan.
9. Cook on 170°C for approximately 40 minutes.
10. As soon as the flan comes out of the oven, brush it with the apple syrup.
11. When the flan has cooled, dust it with icing sugar and enjoy with a dollop of cream.

Suggested drink:

Mug of Red Bush tea.

Illustration using
Jersey Pottery Dragon Fly range

moggy with apple preseve and clotted cream

Serves 8

A moggy is a delicious afternoon tea cake.

for the apple preserve

Ingredients:

500g	bramley apples (or any other acidic apple)
300g	sugar
250ml	mild cider
1	vanilla pod
1	cinnamon stick
7g	pectine
½	lemon zest and juice

Method:
1. Peel and core the apples and cut into segments.
2. Place into a pan and add the cider, cinnamon, lemon juice and finely grated zest.
3. Slit open the vanilla pod to remove the seeds and add all to the apples.
4. Place on stove and heat up gently.
5. Mix sugar and pectine together and add to the apples.
6. Mix well and gently bring to boil.
7. If you use a thermometer, cook to 105°C (like a jam) or otherwise cook for 4 minutes on gentle heat.
8. Fill into clean, sterilised jars and ensure they are airtight.
9. Stand the jars on their lids until the preserve has cooled.

for the moggy

Ingredients:

350g	self-raising flour
½ tsp	salt
2 tsp	ground ginger
160g	butter soft
100g	caster sugar
50g	black treacle
50g	milk

Method:
1. Sift the flour, salt and ginger together into a mixer bowl and add the caster sugar.
2. Rub in the butter.
3. Add the remaining ingredients and bring together to make a dough of scone consistency.
4. Roll out to about 5cm thick and place onto baking paper on a baking tray.
5. Pre-cut into 8 portions and sprinkle with sugar.
6. Cook at 175°C for about 35 minutes.
7. Leave to cool and break into portions.

Suggested drink:

A mug of green tea.

To serve:

Serve the moggy with clotted cream or mascarpone and the preserve.

Illustration using
Jersey Pottery Kate's Cakes range

masterclass:
bread with seeds

700g	strong bread flour
700g	country grain bread flour
743g	water
50g	fresh yeast from the bakery
20g	salt
20g	sugar
20g	Flora margarine
100g	mixed seeds such as sesame, poppy and pumpkin seeds

1. Weigh the flour accurately.
2. Pass the flour through a sieve.
3. Sieving the flour adds air to it and will help the proving process.
4. Add any husk etc. back to the flour.
5. Add the seeds of your choice.
6. Crumble the yeast into the flour.
7. Add salt.
8. Measure the water accurately before adding it to the flour.
9. Now thoroughly mix the ingredients together in a large bowl.
10. Empty the dough out onto the table and work the dough for several minutes until you can feel it becoming elastic.

11. This piece of dough has been resting for at least 30 minutes. Cut the dough into 500g pieces, which will make a small loaf or cake tin.
12. To shape the bread ball, pull the dough in from the sides and fold it into the centre of the dough ball, now press it down to lengthen it slightly.
13. Fit the dough into the prepared tins.
14. Brush the top with water to make the seeds stick.
15. After proving the bread in the tin for about 40 minutes, or until it slightly sticks out of the tin, cook it at about 170°C for approximately 40 minutes.

'crab shack' thick breakfast pancakes served with jersey honey

Makes 20 large pancakes

Ingredients:

150ml   free range eggs
175g   caster sugar
500ml   warm Jersey milk
        (tepid)
550g   flour
15g   fresh yeast
Jersey honey to taste
Jersey crème fraîche
pinch of salt

Method:

1. Mix the yeast with warm milk; it needs to be blood temperature, not too hot, as this will kill the yeast and if it is too cold it will not bring the yeast to life.
2. Whisk the yolks with the sugar, then add the flour. Add the warm milk mixture and then add a pinch of salt. If the batter seems a little thick, add a little extra milk.
3. Cover with cling film and leave in a warm place for about 1 hour until it is light and frothy. Beat the mixture a little and allow it to rest for a further 15 minutes.
4. Heat a non stick pan to a moderate heat and then lightly brush with a little vegetable oil. Going around the pan add a little of the batter. We usually make each pancake at about 2 tablespoons each.
5. Allow to cook for about 2 minutes on the first side then flip them over and cook for another 45 seconds. Dry on a paper towel and serve with Jersey honey or maple syrup.
6. Fresh berries and Jersey crème fraîche can be used as an alternative accompaniment and goes really well with these pancakes.

Suggested drink:

Jersey Pottery special blend Americano coffee.

seed and nine spice cookies

makes about 12 cookies

Ingredients:

460g	plain flour
8g	baking powder
2 tsp	nine spice
350g	butter
160g	oats
1	egg
190g	light brown sugar
150g	almond slivers
40g	pumpkin seeds
40g	sesame nuts
40g	pine nuts
10g	poppy seeds
vanilla essence	

Method:

1. Sift the flour, baking powder and spice together.
2. Combine the butter, sugar and egg to make a paste.
3. Bring all the ingredients together to make the cookie dough.
4. Dust the table lightly with some flour and form a log of 26cm length.
5. Wrap in cling film and leave in fridge for a couple of hours until the dough is firm.
6. Cut into 12 same size discs and place on a sheet of baking paper on an oven tray.
7. Cook at 170°C for about 18 minutes until the centre is cooked.

Chef's tip:

This cookie dough can also be frozen and cut as required.

Suggested drink:

Jersey Pottery special blend latte.

197

jersey butter shortbread

Ingredients:

250g   white flour
250g   Jersey butter
125g   icing sugar
125g   cornflour
lemon essence

Method:
1. Sift the flour and cornflour together.
2. In a bowl mix butter and icing sugar together and add the flour.
3. Mix and knead until it all comes together to a short pastry.
4. Roll out to about 1 inch thick and place onto a baking tray lined with baking paper.
5. Prick with a fork and cook at 165°C for about 25 minutes until cooked and slightly golden.
6. Cut into desired size when still hot from the oven.
7. Leave to cool before you remove it from the tray.

Suggested drink:
Mug of builder's tea!

louis dressing

Ingredients:

360g	mayonnaise
120g	sweet chilli sauce
3 tbsp	spring onions (chopped)
3 tbsp	green pepper (chopped)
1 tbsp	lemon juice
1½ tsp	Worcestershire sauce
¼ tsp	tabasco sauce

Method:

1. Whisk all the ingredients together in a large bowl.
2. A great dressing to serve with the fruits de mer. Especially good to dip your king prawns in!

warm lemon butter

a perfect dip for lobster, crab and prawns

This is a really nice dip for shellfish, and is also nice with a teaspoon of chopped chilli added at the end of the recipe. That version goes particularly well with hot king prawns, but we prefer not to have too much spice when we serve fresh crab and lobster.

The lovely thing about this sauce is the sourness of the lemon and the richness of the butter.

Ingredients:

200g   unsalted Jersey butter
juice of 3 lemons
salt and cracked white pepper

Method:

Over a low heat gently melt the butter. When it is almost melted squeeze in the lemon, season with salt and cracked pepper and keep warm.

mayonnaise

Our theory on mayonnaise:

At the Jersey Pottery we don't make anything with raw egg products, and as such we do not make our own mayonnaise. Tony often uses raw egg when cooking at home but we don't use them with our customers, choosing instead to use pasteurised egg yolks and whites in certain dishes such as hollandaise and dessert recipes that we have adapted over the years.

When the dangers of raw eggs were first highlighted many years ago, we set out to find a good mayonnaise that was already on the market. Given the amount we use, and our desire to find something 'French' style that would go with shellfish I had to find something suitable.

We have pretty much stuck to our original choice, from 15 years ago, but having moved further into the sandwich market and diversified into so many other areas of the catering business, we have had to find alternatives that can be mixed with mustard for some base dishes and chillies, to make our Thai mayonnaise, however, you can't beat home-made mayonnaise, so here is a recipe.

Ingredients:

2	egg yolks
320ml	very mild olive oil or vegetable oil (or a mix of the two)
¼ tsp	Dijon mustard
½ tbsp	white wine vinegar

salt and pepper

Method:

1. Mix the egg yolks with the Dijon mustard and white wine vinegar, salt and pepper.
2. Whisk well and slowly whisk in the oil a few drops at a time. As the mixture starts to take the oil gradually increase the flow to a stream. If the mixture looks too thick and oily, add a drop of water and it should take all of the oil.

peanut, soy and ginger dip

Ingredients:

150g	peanut butter
1 tbsp	caster sugar
1 tsp	grated ginger
1 tsp	chopped red chilli
2 tbsp	soy sauce
1 tsp	lime juice
100ml	coconut milk
1 small handful of coriander leaves	

Ingredients:

1. In a small saucepan bring the coconut milk to the boil. Add the other ingredients and remove from the heat.
2. Season with a little salt if required and blend in a liquidiser.
3. This sauce will last up to 5 days in the refrigerator as long as it is well covered and is best served warm.

soy salad dressing

Ingredients:

30ml	rice vinegar
30ml	lemon juice
20ml	lime juice
60ml	soy sauce
good pinch sugar	

Method:

1. Put all the ingredients into a glass jar and tighten the lid.
2. Shake well.
3. The dressing will keep in the fridge for a week or so.

veal or game stock

Makes just over 1 litre stock

Ingredients:

3 kg	veal/game/beef bones
2 tbsp	vegetable oil
1	carrot (roughly chopped)
1	small onion
1	stick celery (roughly chopped)
1	small leek (roughly chopped)
1	sprig thyme
5	peppercorns
1	bay leaf
2 tbsp	tomato puree
4ltr	water
2	cloves garlic
100ml	red wine
pinch salt	

Method:

1. Brush the bones with 1 tablespoon of the vegetable oil and place on a baking/roasting tray in a preheated oven at 200°C for 30-40 minutes until the bones are brown.
2. In a large saucepan heat the remaining vegetable oil over a moderate heat, add the vegetables and brown. Stir regularly and when the vegetables are quite brown, add the tomato puree and carry on cooking. Browning the tomato puree at this stage will help you get colour for your finished sauce without using gravy browning.
3. Add the bay leaf, peppercorns, thyme, garlic and add a pinch of salt then add the red wine. Cook until the wine has completely evaporated then add the bones and water and bring to the boil.
4. Skim off the impurities then cook for 4-5 hours. If you skim as you cook this will stop the fat from boiling back into the stock. Pass the stock through a sieve.
5. This will keep for 2-3 days in the fridge and also freezes well.

madeira sauce

Ingredients:

1 ltr	veal stock or game stock
200ml	Madeira
100ml	red wine
1	large red onion (sliced)
1	sprig thyme
2	cloves garlic (sliced)
75g	game or beef trimmings (optional)
1 tbsp	olive oil
salt and pepper	

Method:

1. In a saucepan heat the olive oil and add the meat trimmings if you are using them. Add the red onions, garlic and thyme, fry for a few minutes. Add the red wine and half of the Madeira.
2. Season with salt and pepper and reduce until the liquid has almost completely evaporated. Add the stock, bring to the boil and skim the fat and impurities off the top. Simmer until you have approximately 500ml of the liquid left and add the remaining Madeira, and cook for a further 5 minutes.
3. Check the seasoning and pass through a fine sieve.

Chef's tip:

In all of our recipes we say to reduce the wine before adding stock, but with fortified wines such as Madeira, Port and Sherry, it is nice to have a bit of the raw alcohol flavour – especially in a meat sauce! That's the reason why in this recipe we reduce half of the Madeira and add the other half towards the end. This process also works well with quality wines.

It is worth noting that in all of our recipes we use drinkable wine. We never use wine that can't be drunk because when you reduce the wine it intensifies the flavours, for example, if a wine is corked it comes through in the sauce and if a wine is acidic that flavour will also come through when it is poured over the food.

vegetable stock

Ingredients:

1	large onion
1	large leek
1	large carrot
1	stick celery
1	head fennel
2	cloves garlic (sliced)
8	pink peppercorns
10	black peppercorns
1 tbsp	coriander seeds
1	sprig thyme
1	small bunch tarragon
100ml	white wine
1ltr	water
1 tbsp	olive oil
zest of ½ lemon and orange	
good pinch of salt	

Method:

1. Gently sweat the vegetables in the olive oil for a few minutes and then add the white wine. Boil until it is nearly evaporated, add the herbs, salt, peppercorns, zest and coriander seeds. Add the water and bring to the boil.
2. Simmer for half an hour then remove from the heat and leave the vegetables to infuse for 6 hours.
3. Pass the stocks through a sieve.
4. Keep covered and refrigerate for up to 4 days.

chicken stock

Makes just over 2 litres

Ingredients:

1.5kg	chicken bones (chopped up to fit your saucepan)
3 ltr	water
1	small onion (left in large pieces)
1	carrot (left in large pieces)
1	stick celery (left in large pieces)
10	black peppercorns
2	cloves garlic
1	sprig thyme
1	bay leaf
pinch salt	

Method:

1. Place the chicken bones into a saucepan and bring to the boil. Skim all the impurities that have risen to the top away and add the remaining ingredients.
2. Simmer for 4-5 hours. Top up with a little water as it cooks if necessary.
3. Pass through a sieve.
4. This will keep for 2-3 days in the fridge and also freezes well.

Chef's tip:

Freeze the stock in ice cube trays if you have small quantities, it is then easy to take out a few cubes if you need just a little bit.

parsley broth

This is the mix we use to cook our mussels, cockles and clams for the Plateau fruits de mer.

Ingredients:

30ml	olive oil
2 tsp	chopped garlic
2 tsp	chopped shallots
300ml	white wine
1	small bunch flat parsley (chopped)
salt and pepper	

Method:

To cook the mussels:

1. Prepare the mussels by pulling the beard away ensuring the mussels are firmly closed. Rinse well in running water for a few minutes and drain well. (For best results in a Jersey Pottery colander!) Throw away any that are broken or won't stay closed.
2. Heat a saucepan over a moderate to hot heat and add 1 tablespoon of olive oil, add the garlic and the shallots then throw in the mussels. Shake them around the pan then add the white wine and cover with a lid straight away shaking all the time.
3. When all the mussels are open remove them from the heat, add the remaining olive oil and chopped parsley.
4. The mussels are now ready to serve.
5. The mussels should take no more that 5 minutes to cook.

Chef's tip:

Cockles and clams can be cooked in the same way but they will usually need to be soaked in water for an hour and so before they are cooked, due to the way that cockles and clams bury themselves in the sand.
Cockles cook almost as quickly as mussels and the clams need a little more cooking over a slightly more gentle heat once they have opened, which will help to tenderise them.

as a dressing:

It is also a great dressing to make up and pour over the plateau fruits de mer. For this recipe, in a saucepan lightly cook the shallots and garlic in 1 tablespoon of the olive oil, increase the heat and add the white wine. Reduce the liquid until the wine has almost evaporated, remove from the heat, then whisk in the remainder of the olive oil and then add the parsley, pour over the shellfish. If you like an extra kick, you can add some red chillies.

apple chutney – to serve with cheese

Ingredients:

400g   onions (finely chopped)
200ml   white wine vinegar
1 kg   cooking apples
1 tsp   salt
1 tsp   ground ginger
4   cloves garlic
1   pinch nutmeg
150g   sugar
4 tbsp   chopped mint

Method:

1. Cook the onions in the vinegar slowly over a low heat in a stainless steel pan until they are soft. Then add the remaining ingredients – apart from the chopped mint.
2. Cook over a moderate heat until the mixture is thick.
3. Allow the excess liquid to evaporate, remove from the heat and add the chopped mint.
4. Store in a cool place, preferably in a glass kilner jar.
5. If stored properly, this chutney can last for weeks. It is also delicious served with Ploughman's and cured meat platters.

tempura batter

Ingredients:

150g   plain flour
50g   cornflour
1 pinch salt
1 pinch cayenne pepper
1 pinch baking powder
220ml   cold sparkling water
4   ice cubes

Method:

Combine the flour, corn flour and baking powder in a bowl and add the salt and cayenne pepper. Slowly whisk in the water, then add the ice cubes and keep chilled.

garlic mayonnaise

Ingredients:

250ml   basic mayonnaise (see recipe page 200)
2 cloves finely chopped/crushed garlic
3 tbsp   of chopped parsley
1 tsp   of lemon juice

Method:

Mix all of the ingredients together. The garlic mayonnaise will keep in the fridge for up to one week.

ginger sauce for seared fish

Ingredients:

3 tbsp   olive oil
1   head fennel (sliced)
5   shallots (large, peeled and sliced)
60g   fresh root ginger (peeled and sliced)
5   cloves garlic
100ml   white wine
2   star anise
1 sprig rosemary
1 sprig tarragon
10   peppercorns
250ml   chicken stock
100ml   double cream
150g   unsalted butter (diced)
juice of ½ a lemon
salt (for seasoning)

Method:

1. In a heavy based saucepan put the olive oil and heat over a medium heat. Add the shallots, ginger, garlic and fennel and cook for 3 to 4 minutes.
2. Add the star anise, tarragon, peppercorns and rosemary and season with a little salt. Add the white wine and reduce until the liquid is almost completely evaporated, then add the chicken stock and reduce again until there's only a small drop of liquid left.
3. Add the cream, bring to the boil and allow to simmer for 2 to 3 minutes. Whisk the butter in and finish with the lemon juice, if needed.

ingredients, measurements and timings

All spoon measures are level unless otherwise stated: 1 tsp = 5ml spoon; 1 tbsp = 15ml spoon.

Use fresh herbs, sea salt and freshly ground black pepper unless otherwise suggested.

Timings are for fan-assisted ovens. If using a conventional oven, increase the temperature by 15°C (1 Gas mark). Use an oven thermometer to check the temperature.

Fresh, local Jersey produce has been used and recommended throughout this book, however, where Jersey produce is unavailable, we recommend any high-quality, regional produce.

203

Once one of Jersey's most crucial defences, the restored Seymour Tower is an ideal spot for foodies who want to enjoy fresh seafood and discover the marine wilderness of Jersey's coastline

cooking at source

"Look at these Mye I found," says guide Dominic Jones, holding out a handful of wet molluscs – their glistening, tongue-like bodies oozing out of their flat, grey shells. "They'll be lovely grilled with a bit of garlic butter." As anyone on a trip to the island will discover, it's not an unusual thing in Jersey to just stumble across colonies of fresh seafood ripe for the picking.

As you make your way across the shimmering sand towards Seymour Tower, you will spot dozens of clam, crab and cockle shells – evidence of the positively seething marine life surrounding Jersey. On this particular trip, Tony Dorris has a mission: to cook a fresh seafood lunch using ingredients available from within a ten- to 15-minute walk of the tower. This area is a seafood lover's dream – alive with vast communities of sea creatures thriving in this unique organic environment.

"There are lots of towers around the island but this is the most exposed, and the area surrounding it is a nursery for almost every type of European seafish," enthuses Dominic. "In terms of fish that you'd be looking to eat, lobsters are around here at low tide, there are velvet crabs, lots of different types of clams, praire, palourdes, cockles, and then there are sand eels which are up to eight inches long."

These sand eels are something of a local speciality. If you scrape along the sand at low tide you can find them and people fry them up with butter as a tasty snack. Bass is the most aggressive and the most plentiful fish, but there's also mullet, sole, dogfish and plaice – not to mention wild oysters on the rocks, razor clams and shrimps. They say that every square metre of sand in Jersey has the same protein and energy as a Mars bar, which gives some indication of just how rich it is.

Groups looking to indulge in a Seymour Tower experience are obliged to bring a guide with them. Dominic knows more about Seymour Tower than most, thanks to his extensive local knowledge (he grew up on the island) and the fact that he's a fully trained Seymour Tower guide.

It takes about half an hour to make it to the impressive structure and on arrival Tony sets up a

barbecue on the viewing platform which doubles as a patio, then gets to work filleting the big silver bass on the side of the tower's thick wall. He is totally at home with the beach as his kitchen, chopping busily at the parsley, garlic and chilli for the crab linguine.

The big brown crab he's brought with him is soon knocked into a delicious crab linguine – the thin strands of pasta coated in butter, parmesan, chilli, lemon-juice and the nutty, juicy meat of the crab.

While enjoying the barbecued lobster – red with coral and drizzled in garlic and herb butter – Dominic explains that Seymour Tower is one of his favourite places on earth, and, with such a superb location matched with delicious, truly fresh food, it's easy to see why.

great **taste** gold '08

JERSEY BLACK BUTTER

"A unique Jersey speciality.
A mixture of apples, cider, licorice and spices
create a dark rich apple fruit butter.
Perfect on toast!"

MADE AT THE
LA MARE ESTATE, JERSEY

Genuine
jersey

black butter
'Le Niere Buerre'

Black butter is something of a food legend in Jersey.
One of the great products of the island used to be cider,
with many cider-apple orchards to be found all over Jersey
and black butter was largely a by-product of cider making

There are a couple of important points to make about black butter: firstly it contains no butter, the butter in the name being like the cheese in lemon cheese, more a description of the consistency and application of the product than anything else; and second, it is not really black, indeed a great deal of effort goes into avoiding the burning that would change the dark brown mass to black.

Making black butter is a social affair on the island, a community event these days. Particularly in November villages hold 'sethees d'nier beurre', black butter evenings. This too is a misnomer, as the production will last a night and a day.

The product is made in sizeable quantities, a typical pan for the preparation of black butter (a big copper-bottomed or brass affair known locally as a bachin) being over three feet in diameter. This is filled with cider and set to boil, then filled with peeled and sliced apples, predominantly sweet, but with a good sprinkling of more tart varieties thrown in. The lot is simmered slowly, all the while being stirred with a traditional long-handled utensil called a 'rabot' – long-handled for a good reason; the cooking mixture can spit very hot gushes of apple onto the unwary.

The addition of apples goes on for a long time, cooking and thickening for many hours. When the last apples have gone in, they continue cooking for an hour or more before adding pulped whole lemons as an aid to the flavour and the preserving qualities of the butter. When this addition has had time to be assimilated spices are stirred in – allspice, cinnamon and nutmeg are used - along with sticks of black liquorice which have been pounded down to hasten their incorporation in the whole. Sugar is added to sweeten the dish.

There is a traditional method of testing the 'doneness' of the black butter. If a dollop dropped on a plate to cool allows a wooden spoon pressed into it to lift the plate, then it is ready.

Black butter is sold in jars, often of a pound weight, and is used to spread on bread and scones, or it can be eaten as a treat on its own. It is available to purchase from Jersey Pottery and La Mare Wine Estate.

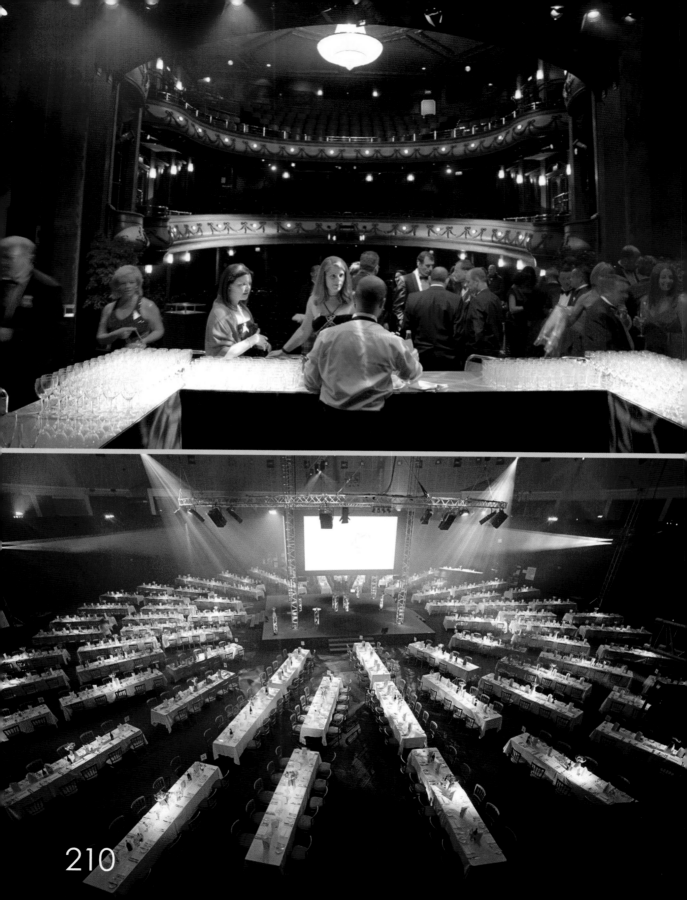

eventful catering

Getting stuck at a deserted castle until 4am, feeding royalty and unveiling surprise ice sculptures: there's never a dull moment in the life of an event caterer

If anyone knows how to throw a party, it's Matthew Jones. In fact, ever since taking over the reigns of the Jersey Pottery Catering & Events arm in 1996, he's made a full time job out of exactly that. "It all started when a friend asked if we could cater their wedding," he says. "They came to us because they liked the food we serve in our restaurants. Then we did our sister's wedding and realised that actually, we could make a whole business out of it."

Fast forward over a decade and Matthew (along with chef director Tony Dorris) is in charge of Jersey's biggest and best-loved event catering operation. In his role he plans and executes hundreds of events a year – catering anything from picnics on the beach with eight people to 800-cover three course sit down meals or state dinners for royalty. It's a high-pressure job that involves a lot of planning, so how does he go about creating an event from scratch?

"We deal with it day by day, but we're all very hands on and support each other," says Matthew. "Though we do suggested menus which most people work off – we offer a totally bespoke service, so we can do whatever our clients want," explains Matthew.

211

"Some people have a very clear idea of what they're after, whereas others have no idea and ask for our input all the way. We've noticed a change in the last few years with more and more people asking us what we think works well, which is nice because it shows that our reputation precedes us."

Matthew stresses that the company can offer as little or as much as people want, and that he works with a vast array of preferences, tastes and budgets. "We'd prefer it if people came to us with a budget, but very often we'll just work from a vague idea. We can get some quite large budgets because we don't just organise food – we can sort out all of the entertainment too."

And what entertainment. Jersey Pottery Catering & Events can lay on anything from string quartets and jazz bands to high profile comedians like Jack Dee and Jimmy Carr. You name it, they've done it – from opera dinners, to parties with illusionists, jugglers and magicians. "We like to create the wow factor with our events, and we're always looking for something new and a bit different because we have regular clients – so we need to exceed expectations.

"We had a dessert extravaganza once when we had one half of the marquee as an elegant, birch decorated dining room and the other as a dance floor with musicians. There was a curtain dividing the two areas and halfway through the night we had a reveal where the curtain went up, and behind the dry ice and lights was this huge ice sculpture with a light bar rising out of it with all the desserts. People gasped as we unveiled it."

Indeed, part of the company's style is to create a 'we don't know what's going to happen next' vibe. But dazzling entertainment or not, Matthew is quick to point out that it's the food that's at the heart of it all. "We might start off with gentle entertainment and build it up to a climax throughout the night, but it all stems from our food and service. That's the crucial thing."

He describes the signature food style of Jersey Pottery Catering & Events as "First class produce, local where at all possible. Our food is not messed around with – it's rustic, but really tasty and it's all about the flavour of the ingredient, not masking the flavour. We use fine cuts of meat and we really use as much local Jersey fish and produce as possible because we want to show off as an island what great produce we have – often people have families coming over from abroad, so it's nice to show off to them."

While the food can be broadly described as modern British – like the food in the Pottery restaurants, Matthew and Tony often have to pander to slightly more exotic tastes. "We get asked to do everything from Moroccan to Indian and New Orleans – we do lots of themes for dinners. We do a lot of catering outdoors among Jersey's castles and ruins, which is more relaxed."

Until, that is, the tides get involved. "One of the most memorable events we've ever done was at Elizabeth castle – the big castle out in the middle of the sea where Sir Walter Raleigh lived. I always laugh when they ask us to do events at a castle that was designed to keep people out. They're a challenge because you have to work with the tides – you've only got a two hour window to get out there and back.

"One event we did there, we put all the guests on a boat at 1am when the party finished, but we obviously had to clean up, and we ended up getting stranded out there until 4am. Then we got the van stuck in the sand and had to find a friendly farmer to help us get it out. It was pretty touch and go but we got out in the end."

If you'd like to throw your own Jersey Pottery style party on dry land, why not try your hand at some of the canapés throughout this book?

index

SOUPS

Watercress soup with poached Jersey Royal Bay oysters and fresh horseradish, 20

Sweet potato, pumpkin and mascarpone soup, 22

Jersey crab chowder, 24

Mexican spiced tortilla soup with Jersey crab and coriander, 26

Chunky chicken, vegetable, pine kernel and ricotta soup, 28

Harira – Moroccan style lamb and vegetable soup, 30

SUSHI

Basic sushi rice and sushi rolls, 32

Fillings, 34

Ginger wasabi mayonnaise, 36

Sushi masterclass, 38

STARTERS AND LIGHT DISHES

Blinis, 40

Jersey asparagus with poached quails' eggs and pecorino sabayon, 42

Royal bay oysters Kenney-Herbert, 46

Grilled oysters with chorizo butter, 48

Oysters with sweet vinegar, cucumber and chilli dip, 50

Mussels with local cider, saffron and Jersey cream, 52

Praires farcies, 54

Jersey spider crab cakes with 'shack attack' sauce, 56

Pottery prawns, 58

Asian fish cakes with mango and chilli salsa, 60

Lightly cured salmon and avocado with fresh tomato and basil dressing, 62

Samosa masterclass, 64

Indian style samosas with a mint yoghurt dip, 66

Grilled Jersey spring vegetables with coriander pistou and yoghurt dressing, 68

Braised chicory with garlic with parsley crust, 70

Goats' cheese, red onion and tomato tart, 72

Scotch quails' eggs with curry mayonnaise, 74

SALADS

Greek style Caesar salad, 78

Cobb salad, 80

FISH AND CRUSTACEANS MAIN DISHES

Jersey crab and saffron aioli, 82

How to dress a crab masterclass, 84

Jersey style seafood salad with garlic and olive oil and lemon yoghurt, 86

Oyster box plateau fruits de mer, 88

Hand dived Jersey scallops with garlic herb butter, crisp smoked pancetta and rocket salad, 90

Hand dived Jersey scallops with butternut squash and crab risotto, 92

Fillet of Jersey sea bass with sweet peppers, grilled squid and lemon dressing, 96

Dover sole and hand dived Jersey scallops with orange and rosemary scented squash, 98

Whole Jersey sea bass baked in a salt crust, 100

Grilled red mullet with saffron risotto and warm tomato dressing, 102

Filled of John Dory with spiced butter sauce and tempura of courgette flower stuffed with wild mushrooms, 104

Jersey brill baked in banana leaf served with nam jim dressing and white radish and cucumber salad, 106

Fillet of turbot with coriander, ginger and lentil sauce, 108

Fillet of smoked haddock with leek and potato broth, 110

Smoked fish and shellfish pie with potato and Jersey cheddar, 112

Jersey style fish stew with saffron mashed potato, 114

BARBECUE PRINCIPLES AND DISHES

BBQ fillets of Jersey black bream with twice cooked fennel and salsa verdi, 116-117

Jersey lobster served with raspberry vinegar dressed salad and garlic mayonnaise, 118

Sirloin of beef with chilli rub and balsamic salad served with Jersey royals, 120

Jersey fish with fragrant green curry sauce, 122

Barbecued poussin with lemon paprika and cumin, 124

Beef satay skewers with peanut, soy and ginger dip, 126

POULTRY, GAME AND MEAT MAIN DISHES

Crispy fried duck breast with chicory and watercress salad and citrus and soy dressing, 128

Roast loin of venison with spiced red cabbage and chestnut crumbs, 130

Fillet of pork with white bean and white truffle flavour mash, sauté spinach and Madeira sauce, 132

Jersey Pottery Yorkshire puddings made with beer, 134

Spicy tempura of baby back ribs with ginger dipping sauce, 136

Thai style coconut and peanut beef curry, 138

Slow pot roast leg of lamb with rosemary and garlic, served with milky mashed potatoes, 140

Meatballs with tomato and basil, 142

PASTA DISHES

Basic pasta, 144

Crab ravioli masterclass, 145

Tortellini masterclass, 146

Pigeon and porcini tortellini, 148

Crab and ginger ravioli, 150

CHEESE

Cheese presentation, 152

Oatmeal biscuits, 154

DESSERTS

Poached pear with chocolate pavlova, 156

Pink grapefruit and cinnamon posset, 158

Rum and raisin crème brûlée, 160

Passion fruit and ginger panna cotta, 162

Lime and vodka parfait, 164

Roasted apple parfait, 166

Cheeky raspberry meringue tart, 168

Mille-feuilles of poached apples and brandy snap biscuits, 170

Jersey black butter cheesecake, 172

Saucy helene pear tart, 174

Orange charlotte, 176

White chocolate bavarois with fresh berries, 178

Valrhona chocolate truffles, 180

Doughnuts with gooey chocolate sauce and Jersey vanilla ice cream, 182

Retro walnut tart with Baileys cream, 184

Dragon fly apple flan, 186

Moggy with apple preserve and clotted cream, 188

Bread with seeds masterclass, 190

'Crab shack' thick breakfast pancakes served with Jersey honey, 194

Seed and nine spice cookies, 196

Jersey butter shortbread, 198

STOCKS, SAUCES AND DRESSINGS

Louis dressing, 200

Warm lemon butter, 200

Mayonnaise, 200

Peanut, soy and ginger dip, 200

Soy salad dressing, 200

Veal or game stock, 201

Madeira sauce, 201

Vegetable stock, 201

Chicken stock, 202

Parsley broth, 202

Apple chutney – to serve with cheese, 203

Tempura batter, 203

Garlic mayonnaise, 203

Ginger sauce for seared fish, 203